U.S. Department of Justice
Office of Justice Programs
Bureau of Justice Statistics

I0410782

Policing and Homicide, 1976-98: Justifiable Homicide by Police, Police Officers Murdered by Felons

March 2001,

U.S. Department of Justice
Bureau of Justice Statistics

Lawrence A. Greenfeld
Acting Director

This report was prepared by Jodi M.
Brown and Patrick A. Langan of the
Bureau of Justice Statistics. Matthew
Durose and Donna Oliphant assisted
with verification. Tina Dorsey and Tom
Hester edited and produced the report.
Jayne Robinson prepared the report for
printing.

Frankie Kelley of the Federal Bureau
of Investigation provided tabulations
of LEOKA data specially for this report.

Staff members of the Criminal Justice
Information Services Division of the
Federal Bureau of Investigation read
drafts of this report and responded with
many helpful comments.

Police departments in the following
cities contributed valuable descriptions
of actual cases of justifiable homicide
by police in 1996: Atlanta, Baltimore,
Cleveland, Houston, Los Angeles, New
York City, Oklahoma City, and
Philadelphia.

The data and the report, as well as
others from the Bureau of Justice
Statistics, are available through the
Internet —

http://www.ojp.usdoj.gov/bjs/

Highlights

This report brings together in a single publication national statistics on two distinct types of homicide: the justifiable homicide of felons by police, and the murder of police officers by felons. Although the two are fundamentally different — the use of deadly force against a police officer is almost never justified, while the use of deadly force by police often is — certain connections can be made between them beyond the fact that both always involve the police. Sometimes one directly results in the other: 1 in 6 murders of a police officer result in the justifiable killing of the murderer. (Still, of all the justifiable homicides by police only about 3% occur in connection with the murder of a police officer.) The two also share demographic similarities. For example, almost all the felons justifiably killed by police (98%) and almost all of the felons who murdered a police officer (97%) are males; in both types of homicide just over half of the felons are ages 18 to 30; and in both types just over half of the felons are white.

	Percent of felons killed by police in justifiable homicides, 1976-98	Percent of felons who murdered police officers, 1976-98
Male	98%	97%
Ages 18-30	53%	54%
White	56%	54%
Black	42%	43%
Young white males	16%	20%*
Young black males	16%	21%*

*Percent is for 1980-98.

The first section of the report deals with the justifiable homicide of felons by police; the second, with the murder of police officers by felons. Together, the two types account for around 2% of all intentional killings in the United States. The types of homicide not covered in this report are: negligent homicides; justifiable homicides by private citizens; and murders in which the victim is someone other than an officer slain in the line of duty.

Justifiable homicide by police, 1976-98

In this report, killings by police are referred to as "justifiable homicides," and the persons that police kill are referred to as "felons." These terms reflect the view of the police agencies that provide the data used in this report.

The killing of a felon by police is considered justified when it is done to prevent imminent death or serious bodily injury to the officer or another person. Police justifiably kill on average nearly 400 felons each year (the figure below and figure 1).

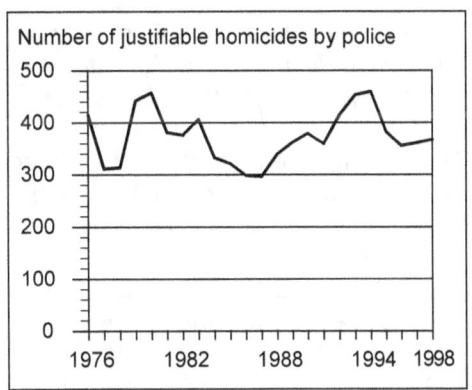

Number of justifiable homicides by police

From 1976 to 1998, the U.S. population age 13 or older grew by about 47 million people and the size of the police force in the United States grew by over 200,000 officers, but the number of felons justifiably killed by police did not generally rise.

A growing percentage of felons killed by police are white, and a declining percentage are black (figure 4).

	Race of felons killed	
1978	50% White	49% Black
1988	59% White	39% Black
1998	62% White	35% Black

Felons justifiably killed by police represent a tiny fraction of the total population. Of the 183 million whites in 1998, police killed 225; of the 27 million blacks, police killed 127. While the rate (per million population) at which blacks were killed by police in 1998 was about 4 times that of whites (the figure below and figure 5), the difference used to be much wider: the black rate in 1978 was 8 times the white rate.

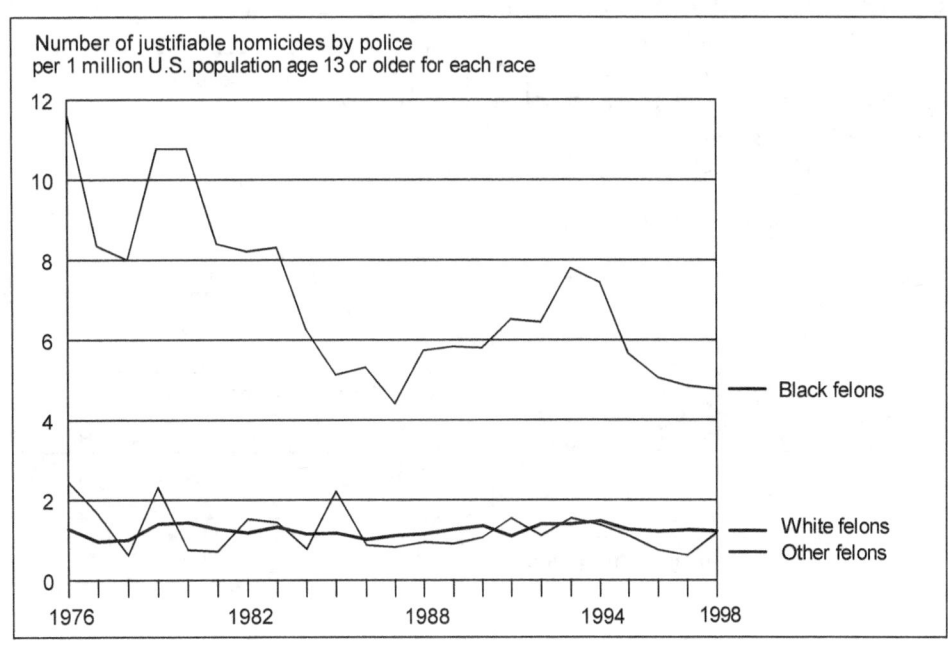

Number of justifiable homicides by police per 1 million U.S. population age 13 or older for each race

Black felons

White felons
Other felons

The highest rates of justifiable homicide are of young black males. Of the Nation's 3.4 million young black males (black males under age 25) in 1998, 48 were justifiably killed by police. That year, young black males made up 1% of the total U.S. population but 14% of felons justifiably killed by police. By comparison, of the Nation's 18.3 million young white males, 53 were justifiably killed. Young white males were 7% of the population and 15% of those killed in 1998.

Of all the felons justifiably killed by police from 1976 to 1998, 53% were ages 18 to 30, and 98% were males.

According to the latest statistics (1998), white officers are 87% of the Nation's police force and account for 82% of justifiable homicides by police. Black officers make up 11% of the Nation's police and account for 17% of the justifiable homicides (figure 10).

Police officers murdered by felons, 1976-98

Since 1976, an average of 79 police officers have been murdered each year in the line of duty (figure 12). The number of officers murdered each year is dropping, and the rate at which police officers are being murdered is steadily falling (the figure below and figure 14).

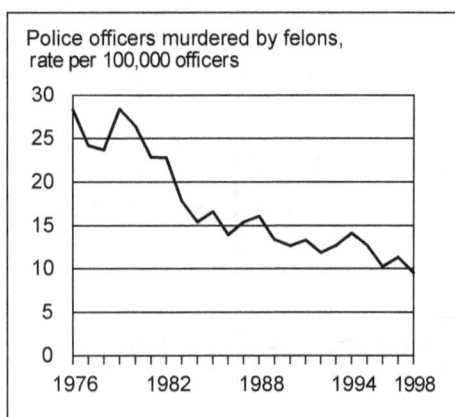

Police officers murdered by felons, rate per 100,000 officers

In 1978, 1 in 4,000 police officers were murdered; in 1988, 1 in 6,000; and in 1998, 1 in 11,000 officers (figure 14).

Throughout much of the 1990's, white police officers made up about 87% of all police officers in the United States and 83% of all officers murdered by felons. Black officers were 11% of police officers but 15% of those murdered. Officers of other races were 2% of police officers and 2% of those murdered (figure 15).

On average, officers murdered from 1976 to 1998 had 9 years of law enforcement service.

From 1976 to 1998, two-thirds of the felons who murdered a police officer had a prior criminal arrest (figure 16).

The majority of police officers murdered by felons were killed while responding to disturbance calls (16%) or arrest situations (39%).

Firearms claimed the lives of 92% of the officers killed in the line of duty from 1976 to 1998. The officer's own gun was used in 12% of all murders of police officers.

Murderers of police officers represent a tiny fraction of the total population. Of the Nation's 18.3 million young white males (white males under age 25), 17 murdered a police officer in 1998. Of the 3.4 million young black males, 13 murdered an officer that year.

From 1980 to 1998, young black males made up about 1% of the U.S. population but 21% of felons who murdered a police officer (figure 17); young white males were 8% of the population but 20% of the murderers of law enforcement officers. Young black males murdered police officers at a rate almost 6 times that of young white males (5.7 versus 1 per million population) (the figure below and figure 18).

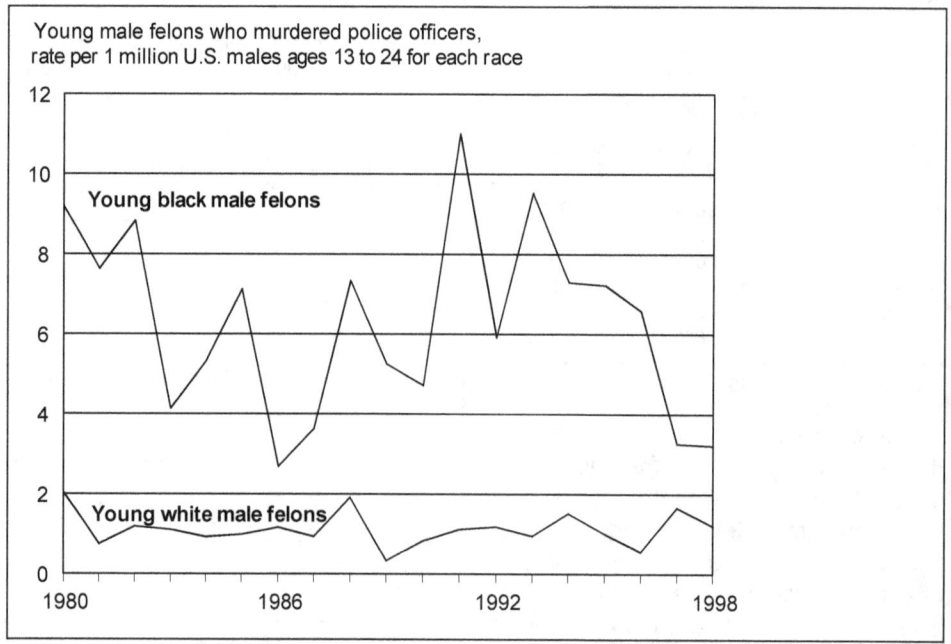

Young male felons who murdered police officers, rate per 1 million U.S. males ages 13 to 24 for each race

Young black male felons

Young white male felons

Contents

Justifiable homicide by police, 1976-98

When a police officer deliberately kills someone, a determination is made as to whether the homicide occurred in the line of duty and whether the homicide was justified to prevent imminent death or serious bodily injury to the officer or another person. If an investigation determines that the homicide did occur in the line of duty and that circumstances did warrant lethal force, a record of a justifiable homicide is voluntarily sent by the officer's agency to the FBI in Washington. Each record of justifiable homicide received is then entered into a database.

The database contains such information as the felon's age, race, and gender, and such information on the officer as age, race, and gender.

In this report, killings by police are referred to as "justifiable homicides," and the persons that police kill are referred to as "felons." These terms reflect the view of the police agencies that provide the data used in this report.

Annual trends in justifiable homicides by police

Though the FBI database has records of justifiable homicides by police from 1968, this report is concerned just with homicides occurring since 1976 (see *Methodology* page 28). The records since 1976 have fuller information than earlier records, including information not only on the felons, but also on the police officers.

According to FBI national data on justifiable homicides by police from 1976 to 1998 —

• 8,578 felons were justifiably killed by police in the United States.

• The largest number of recorded justifiable homicides in a single year was 459 (in 1994), and the smallest number was 296 (in 1987) (figure 1).

• On average 373 felons were lawfully killed by police each year.

• From 1976 to 1998, the U.S. population age 13 or older grew by about 47 million people and the size of the police force in the United States grew by over 200,000 officers, but the number of felons justifiably killed by police did not generally rise.

• On average each year about 2 persons per 1 million residents age 13 or older were justifiably killed by law enforcement officers (figure 2). (Because police rarely kill someone under age 13, the rate calculation is per 1 million U.S. population age 13 or older.)

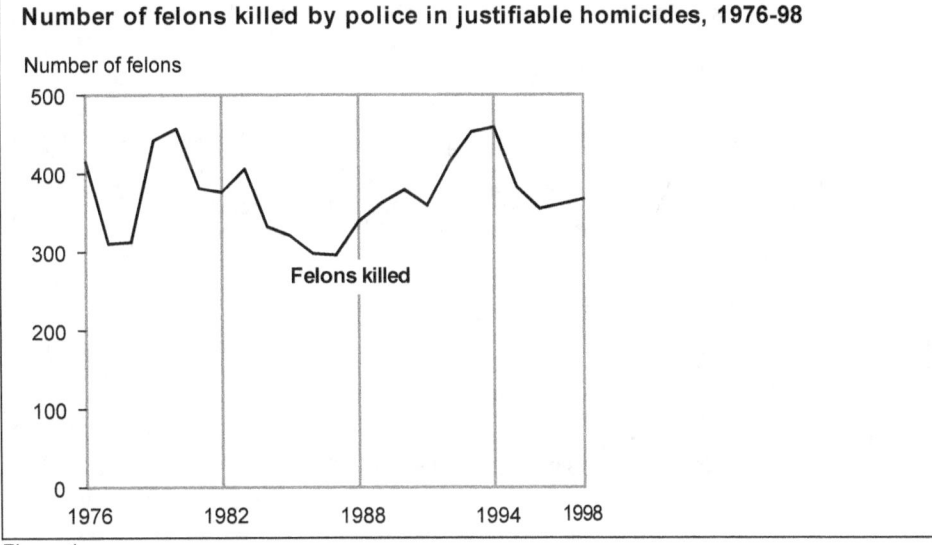

Number of felons killed by police in justifiable homicides, 1976-98

Number of felons

Felons killed

Figure 1

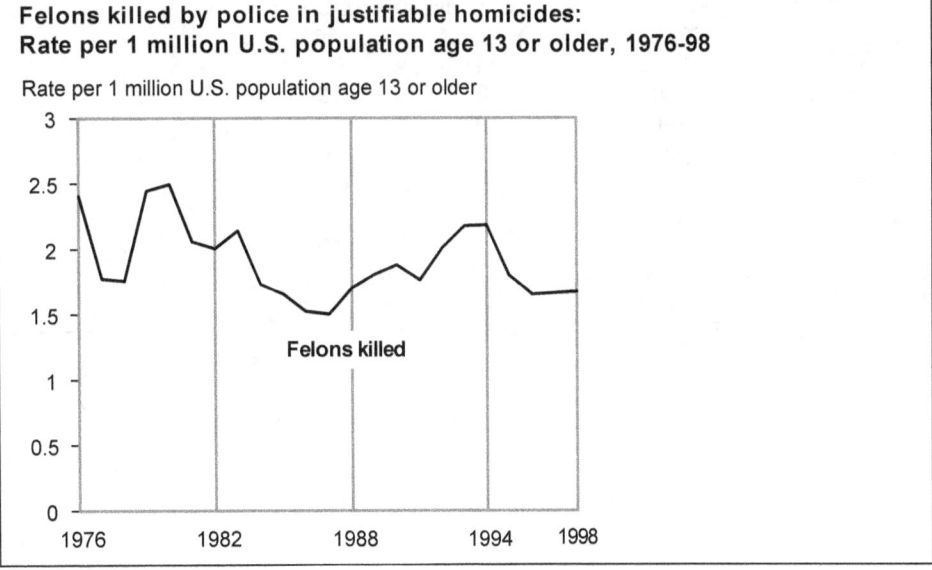

Felons killed by police in justifiable homicides: Rate per 1 million U.S. population age 13 or older, 1976-98

Rate per 1 million U.S. population age 13 or older

Felons killed

Figure 2

Throughout this report, the national statistics given on justifiable homicides by police were "unadjusted," meaning no correction was made for the fact that some States did not report to the FBI any of the justifiable homicides that occurred in certain years. For example, Florida did not report in 1988, and so the national total of 339 justifiable homicides in 1988 is missing whatever number of justifiable homicides occurred in Florida that year.

To illustrate what effect missing States might have, unadjusted and adjusted rates of justifiable homicide were plotted on the same graph (below). In calculating unadjusted rates, missing States were treated as having no justifiable homicides; in adjusted rates, missing States were treated as having the same number of justifiable homicides they had reported in the closest preceding year. For example, Florida submitted no data for 1988 but did report 24 justifiable homicides in 1987. The 1988 adjusted national rate therefore includes an estimated 24 Florida homicides.

Rates of felons killed by police in justifiable homicides

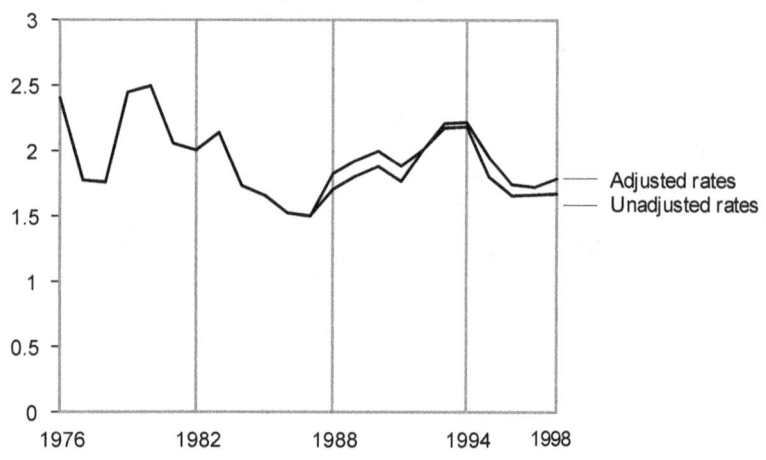

Adjusted year(s)	Missing State	Estimate used to calculate adjusted rate	
		Number	Year
1988-91	Florida	24	1987
1997-98	Florida	6	1996
1988	Kentucky	0	1987
1993-98	Kansas	7	1992
1995	Illinois	25	1994
1996	D.C.	12	1995
1998	D.C.	7	1997
1998	Wisconsin	5	1997

Table 1. Felons killed by police in justifiable homicides: Percent killed with firearms, 1976-98

Year	Total number of justifiable homicides	Percent with firearms
Annual average	373	99.0%
1976	415	99.8%
1977	311	99.0
1978	313	99.7
1979	442	98.9
1980	457	98.9%
1981	381	98.7
1982	376	96.8
1983	406	99.5
1984	332	98.5
1985	321	98.4%
1986	298	99.0
1987	296	99.0
1988	339	98.8
1989	362	99.2
1990	379	99.2%
1991	359	98.6
1992	414	98.3
1993	453	99.6
1994	459	99.8
1995	382	99.2%
1996	355	98.3
1997	361	99.4
1998	367	99.5

Note: "Total number" includes all instances of justifiable homicide by police whether or not the type of weapon used is known. The type of weapon is known in 99.9% of the justifiable homicides committed by police between 1976 and 1998.
Source: FBI database, *Supplementary Homicide Reports.*

Table 2. Gender of felons killed by police in justifiable homicides, 1976-98

Year	Total number of justifiable homicides	Percent of killed felons Male	Female
Annual average	373	98%	2%
1976	415	99%	1%
1977	311	98	2
1978	313	98	2
1979	442	97	3
1980	457	98%	2%
1981	381	99	1
1982	376	98	2
1983	406	99	1
1984	332	98	2
1985	321	98%	2%
1986	298	99	1
1987	296	98	2
1988	339	98	2
1989	362	96	4
1990	379	97%	3%
1991	359	96	4
1992	414	98	2
1993	453	97	3
1994	459	96	4
1995	382	99%	1%
1996	355	98	2
1997	361	97	3
1998	367	98	2

Note: "Total number" includes all instances of justifiable homicide by police whether or not the demographic characteristics are known. The felon's gender is known in 99.9% of the justifiable homicides by police between 1976 and 1998.
Source: FBI database, *Supplementary Homicide Reports.*

• Police used a firearm (usually a handgun) in 99% of justifiable homicides (table 1). In many cases where police killed a felon with a firearm, the felon was shot multiple times. This is consistent with police training. When police have to shoot, they will keep shooting until the felon no longer poses a threat.

Felons killed by police in justifiable homicides

Persons justifiably killed by police are referred to in the FBI's national database as "felons" because, at the time of the homicide, they were involved (or were thought to be involved) in a violent felony. The demographic information available on them in the database is their gender, race, and age.

Of the 8,578 felons killed by police from 1976 to 1998, 98% of them had all 3 of their demographic characteristics recorded in the database.

According to FBI national data on justifiable homicides by police from 1976 to 1998 —

Felons' gender

• 98% of persons justifiably killed by police were males (table 2).

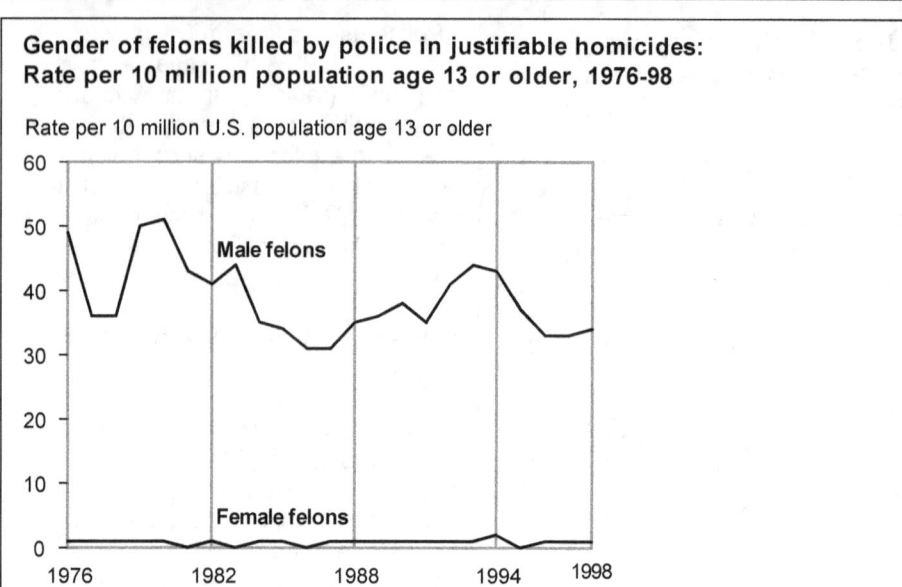

Gender of felons killed by police in justifiable homicides: Rate per 10 million population age 13 or older, 1976-98

Rate per 10 million U.S. population age 13 or older

Figure 3

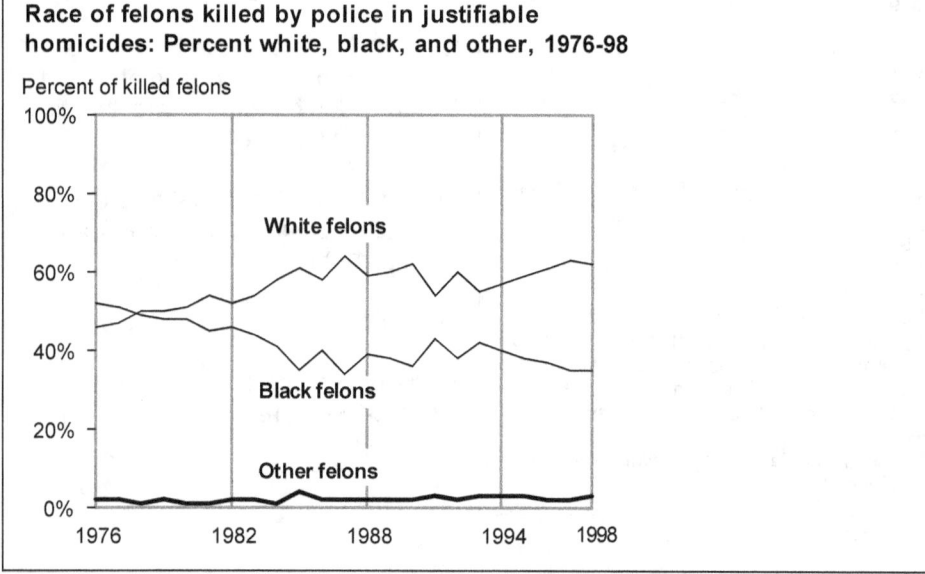

Race of felons killed by police in justifiable homicides: Percent white, black, and other, 1976-98

Percent of killed felons

Figure 4

• Males were slain by police in justifiable homicides at a rate almost 40 times that of females (39 deaths of males per 10 million male residents versus 1 death per 10 million female residents) (figure 3).

• In 1998, males made up 48% of the population age 13 or older, but accounted for 83% of persons arrested for violent crime and 98% of felons killed by police. The 1998 statistics illustrate both the comparatively high rate of justifiable homicide involving males and the similarity between persons arrested by police and felons killed by police.

Felons' race

• Most felons killed by police each year were white (except for 1976 and 1977) (figure 4).

• A growing percentage of felons killed by police are white, and a declining percentage are black.

	Race of felons killed	
1978	50% white	49% black
1988	59% white	39% black
1998	62% white	35% black

Race of felons killed by police in justifiable homicides: Rate per 1 million U.S. population age 13 or older, 1976-98

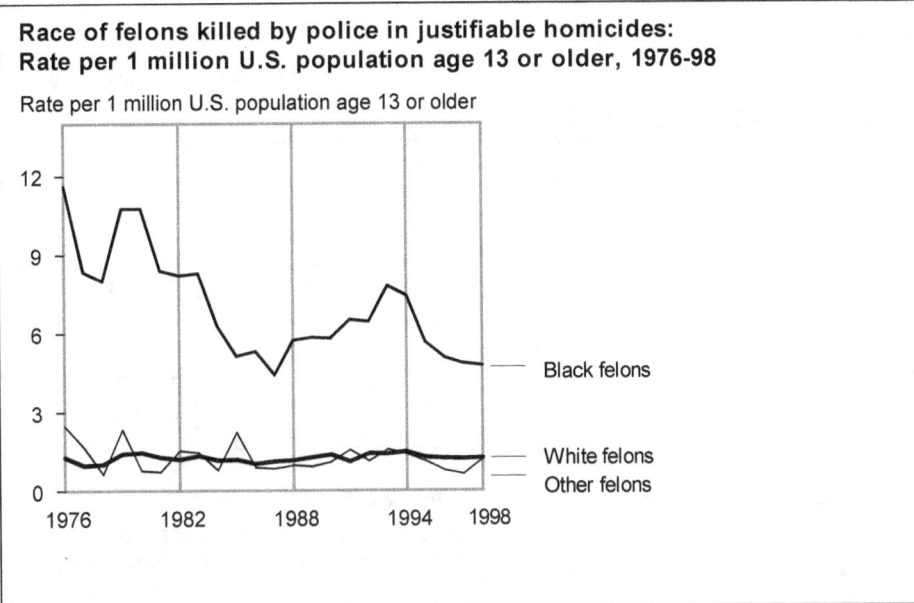

Rate per 1 million U.S. population age 13 or older

Figure 5

Rates of arrest for violent crime (per 10,000) and justifiable homicide by police (per 10,000,000) age 13 or older, 1976-98

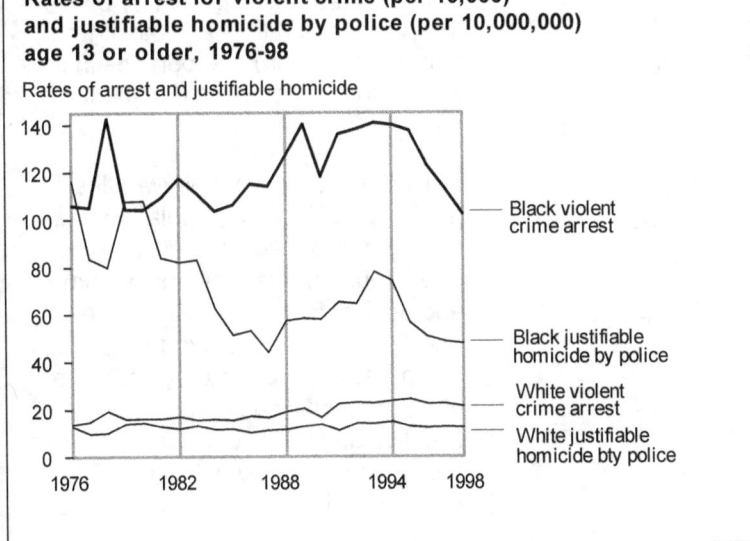

Rates of arrest and justifiable homicide

Figure 6

• In 1998 blacks made up 12% of the population age 13 or older but accounted for 40% of persons arrested for violent crime and 35% of felons killed by police. The 1998 statistics illustrate both the comparatively high rate of justifiable homicide involving blacks and the racial similarity between persons arrested by police and felons killed by police.

• Felons justifiably killed by police represent a tiny fraction of the total population. Of the 183 million whites in 1998, police killed 225; of the 27 million blacks, police killed 127. While the rate (per million population) at which blacks were killed in 1998 was about 4 times that of whites, the difference used to be much wider: the black rate in 1978 was 8 times the white rate (figure 5).

• The rate at which blacks are killed by police in justifiable homicides is declining, while the rate at which whites are killed by police shows no consistent trend.

	Rate of justifiable homicide by police (per 1 million population)	
	White	Black
1978	1.0	8.0
1988	1.2	5.7
1998	1.2	4.8

Correlation with arrest for violent crime

• There is little correspondence between trends in arrests for violent crimes and trends in justifiable homicides by police (the correlation is +0.2 for whites and -0.2 for blacks) (figure 6).

Table 3. Age of felons killed by police in justifiable homicides, 1976-98

Year	Total number of justifiable homicides	Percent of killed felons who were ages —					
		13-19	20-24	25-29	30-34	35-39	40 or older
Annual average	373	11%	21%	21%	17%	11%	19%
1976	415	15%	25%	25%	13%	8%	14%
1977	311	12	23	21	13	10	21
1978	313	14	25	17	13	11	20
1979	442	13	25	21	15	9	17
1980	457	11%	27%	22%	17%	11%	12%
1981	381	12	21	26	15	10	16
1982	376	10	22	26	17	9	16
1983	406	8	20	21	19	9	23
1984	332	10	22	21	16	10	21
1985	321	7%	22%	25%	15%	11%	20%
1986	298	10	18	22	21	11	18
1987	296	7	21	19	16	14	23
1988	339	10	16	26	19	11	18
1989	362	9	19	23	19	10	20
1990	379	9%	19%	22%	17%	12%	21%
1991	359	15	20	22	18	9	16
1992	414	13	22	21	16	11	17
1993	453	14	20	17	16	11	22
1994	459	12	21	17	17	13	20
1995	382	13%	22%	15%	20%	12%	18%
1996	355	13	19	17	19	11	21
1997	361	11	17	18	17	15	22
1998	367	12	18	18	16	12	24

Note: "Total number" includes all instances of justifiable homicide by police whether or not the demographic characteristics are known. The felon's age is known in 98.7% of the justifiable homicides by police between 1976 and 1998. The 13-19 age category includes one 11-year-old in 1981 and one 12-year-old in 1992.
Source: FBI database, *Supplementary Homicide Reports*.

Age of felons killed by police in justifiable homicides: Rate per 1 million population, 1976-98

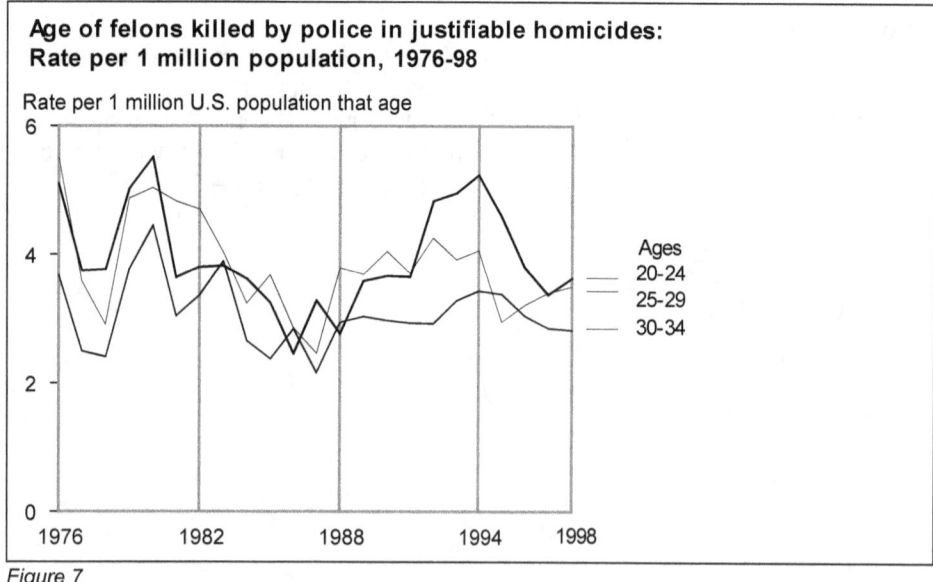

Figure 7

• Except for an 11-year-old killed by police in 1981 and a 12-year-old in 1992, all persons slain by police in justifiable homicides from 1976 to 1998 were in their teens or older.

• The average age of felons justifiably killed by police from 1976 to 1998 was 31 years.

• Felons ages 18 to 30 (not shown in table 3) were 53% of justifiable homicides by police from 1976 to 1998.

• In most years, felons in their twenties accounted for more justifiable homicides than any other age categories (table 3).

• Persons in their twenties had the highest rates of being slain by police in justifiable homicides (almost 4 per million population) and persons in their early thirties had the next highest rate (figure 7).

• In 1998 persons in their twenties made up 16% of the population age 13 or older, but accounted for 31% of persons arrested for violent crime and 36% of felons killed by police. The 1998 statistics illustrate both the comparatively high rate of justifiable homicide involving persons in their twenties and the age similarity between persons arrested by police and felons killed by police.

• According to latest statistics (1998), the average age of felons killed by police is 32, and half are age 30 or older.

Felons' gender and race

• The vast majority of felons killed by police each year (about 96%) are either white males or black males (table 4).

• Of the felons killed by police from 1976 to 1998, 55% were white males, 41% were black males, 1% were white females, 1% were black females, and the rest were mostly males in the "other races" category (Asian, Pacific Islander, Alaska Native, and American Indian).

• Felons justifiably killed by police represent a tiny fraction of the total population. Of the 89 million white males (age 13 or older) in 1998, police killed 220; of the 12 million black males (age 13 or older), police killed 125. In 1998 black males were around 6% of the general population (age 13 or older) but 34% of persons killed by police, and white males were 41% of the general population (age 13 or older) but 61% of those killed.

• Among persons killed by police, white males outnumbered black males.

Percent of all felons killed by police
1978 48% white males   49% black males
1988 57% white males   39% black males
1998 61% white males   34% black males

Table 4. Gender and race of felons killed by police in justifiable homicides, 1976-98

Year	Total number of justifiable homicides	Percent of killed felons who were —							
		Male				Female			
		Total	White	Black	Other	Total	White	Black	Other
Annual average	373	98%	55%	41%	2%	2%	1%	1%	0%
1976	415	99%	46%	51%	2%	1%	1%	0%	0%
1977	311	98	47	49	2	2	0	2	0
1978	313	98	48	49	1	2	1	1	0
1979	442	97	49	47	2	3	1	2	0
1980	457	98%	50%	47%	1%	2%	1%	1%	0%
1981	381	99	54	44	1	1	0	1	0
1982	376	98	51	46	2	2	1	1	0
1983	406	99	54	44	2	1	0	1	0
1984	332	98	56	40	1	2	2	1	0
1985	321	98%	59%	35%	4%	2%	2%	1%	0%
1986	298	99	57	40	2	1	1	0	0
1987	296	98	63	33	2	2	1	1	0
1988	339	98	57	39	2	2	2	0	0
1989	362	96	58	36	2	4	2	2	0
1990	379	97%	61%	34%	2%	3%	1%	2%	0%
1991	359	96	51	42	3	4	2	1	1
1992	414	98	58	38	2	2	2	0	0
1993	453	97	53	41	3	3	2	1	0
1994	459	96	54	39	3	4	3	1	0
1995	382	99%	59%	37%	3%	1%	1%	0%	0%
1996	355	98	60	36	2	2	2	1	0
1997	361	97	61	34	2	3	2	1	0
1998	367	98	61	34	3	2	1	1	0

Note: "Total number" includes all instances of justifiable homicide by police, whether or not the gender and race are known. The felon's gender and race are both known in 99.3% of the justifiable homicides by police between 1976 and 1998.
Due to rounding error, detail may not sum to total.
Source: FBI database, *Supplementary Homicide Reports*.

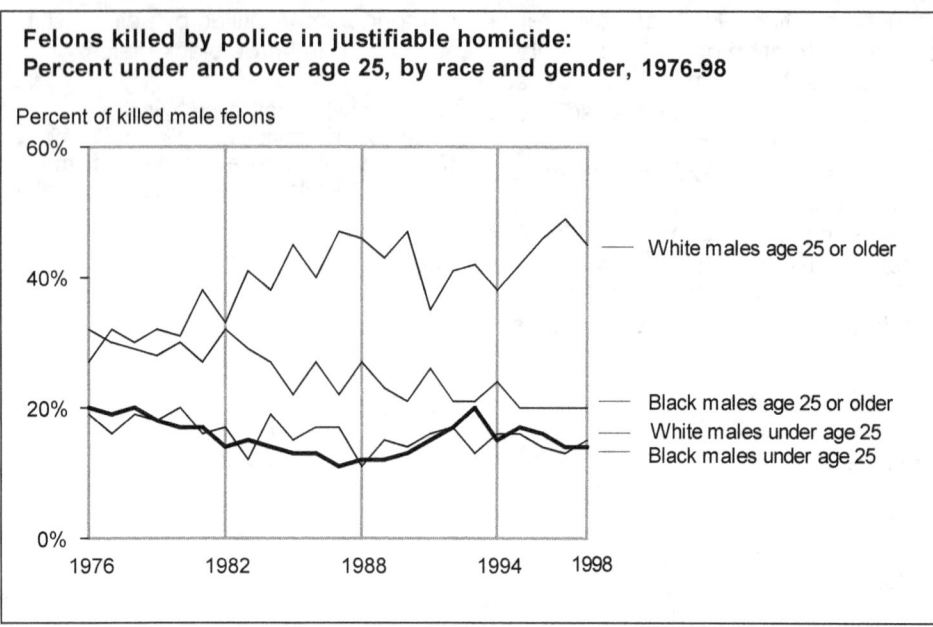

Felons killed by police in justifiable homicide: Percent under and over age 25, by race and gender, 1976-98

Percent of killed male felons

- White males age 25 or older
- Black males age 25 or older
- White males under age 25
- Black males under age 25

Figure 8

Felons' gender, race, and age

• The highest rates of justifiable homicide are of young black males. Of the Nation's 3.4 million young black males (black males under age 25) in 1998, 48 were justifiably killed by police. That year, young black males made up 1% of the total U.S. population but 14% of felons justifiably killed by police. By comparison, of the Nation's 18.3 million young white males, 53 were justifiably killed. Young white males were 8% of the population and 15% of those killed in 1998.

• From 1976 to 1998 young black males (black males under age 25) made up about 1% of the population but 16% of felons killed by police in justifiable homicides; young white males made up about 8% of the population but 16% of felons killed by police (figure 8).

• Of all felons justifiably killed by police from 1976 to 1998, the majority were young white males under age 25 (16%), young black males under age 25 (16%), white males age 25 or older (39%), and black males age 25 or older (25%).

• From 1980 to 1998 young black males were killed by police in justifiable homicides at a rate approximately 6 times that of young white males (16.5 versus 2.9 per million population) (figure 9).

• Average ages of felons killed by police from 1976 to 1998 were —

Race	Males	Females
White	32 yrs	35 yrs
Black	29	39
Other	29	33

• Median ages of felons killed by police from 1976 to 1998 were —

Race	Males	Females
White	30 yrs	33 yrs
Black	27	36
Other	27	33

• White and black males ages 20 to 34 made up most of the felons killed by police (56%) from 1976 to 1998.

• Based on latest statistics (1998), together white males and black males ages 20 to 34 are 10% of the general population but 48% of those killed by police.

• Latest statistics (1998) indicate that white males ages 20 to 34 are 8% of the general population but 29% of those killed by police, and black males ages 20 to 34 are 1.4% of the general population but 20% of persons killed by police in justifiable homicides.

Officers who killed felons in justifiable homicides

The police officer's gender, race, and age are a part of the record for each justifiable homicide entered into the national database, but since participation is voluntary, police agencies do not always supply this information. There were 8,578 felons killed by police from 1976 to 1998. The age, race, and gender of the officer involved in the homicide were recorded on 69% of them, and at least one of the three characteristics was recorded on 85%.

According to FBI national data on justifiable homicides by police from 1976 to 1998 —

Officers' gender

• The officer in a justifiable homicide case is almost always a male (98%) (table 5).

Table 5. Gender of police officers who killed felons in justifiable homicides: Percent male and female, 1976-98

Year	Total number of justifiable homicides by police	Percent of officers Male	Female
Annual average	373	98%	2%
1976	415	99%	1%
1977	311	98	2
1978	313	99	1
1979	442	99	1
1980	457	99%	1%
1981	381	99	1
1982	376	98	2
1983	406	98	2
1984	332	99	1
1985	321	97%	3%
1986	298	99	1
1987	296	96	4
1988	339	97	3
1989	362	98	2
1990	379	97%	3%
1991	359	98	2
1992	414	98	2
1993	453	98	2
1994	459	99	1
1995	382	98%	2%
1996	355	98	2
1997	361	97	3
1998	367	97	3

Note: "Total number" includes all instances of justifiable homicide by police whether or not the demographic characteristics are known. The officer's gender is known in 84.8% of the justifiable homicides by police between 1976 and 1998.
Source: FBI database, *Supplementary Homicide Reports.*

Young male felons killed by police in justifiable homicides: Rate per 1 million young white and black males, 1980-98

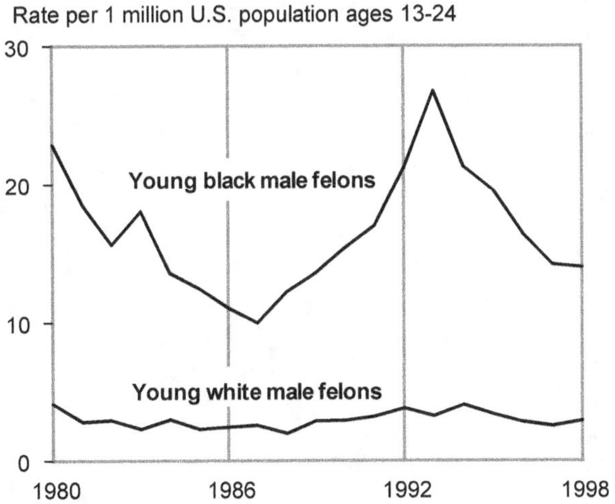

Rate per 1 million U.S. population ages 13-24

Figure 9

Race of police officers who killed felons in justifiable homicides: Percent white and black, 1976-98

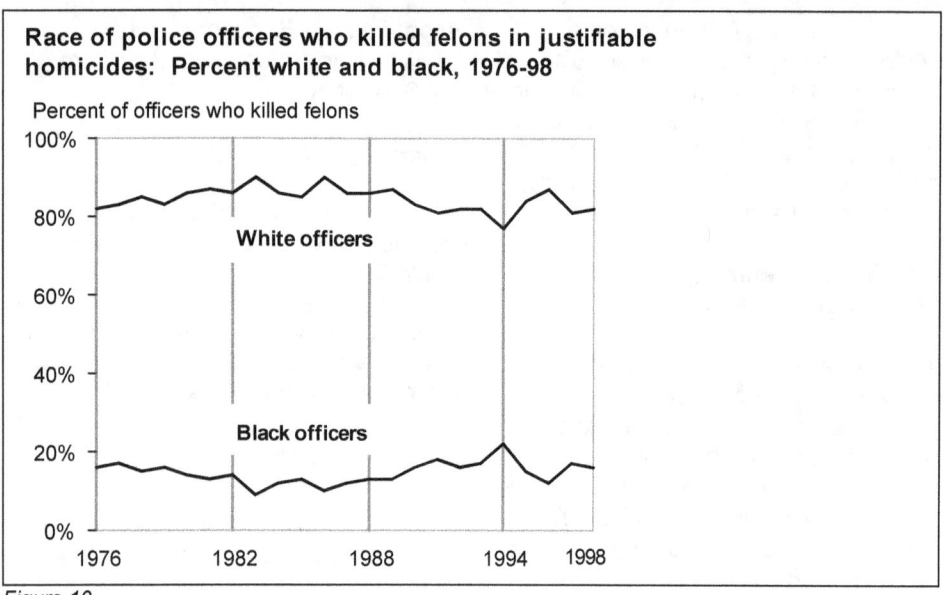

Figure 10

Officers' race

• From 1976 to 1998 the officer in 84% of justifiable homicides by police was white, and the officer in 15% was black (figure 10).

Officers' age

• In most years officers ages 25 to 29 accounted for more justifiable homicides than any other age category (table 6).

• The average age of the officer in a justifiable homicide by police was 33 years.

• 55% of officers in justifiable homicides were over age 30 (not shown in table 6).

Table 6. Age of police officers who killed felons in justifiable homicides, 1976-98

Year	Total number of justifiable homicides by police	Percent of officers who were ages —					
		Under 20	20-24	25-29	30-34	35-39	40 or older
Annual average	373	1%	9%	28%	28%	17%	17%
1976	415	0%	10%	37%	30%	10%	13%
1977	311	0	11	39	28	10	12
1978	313	1	13	35	32	12	7
1979	442	0	9	30	29	16	16
1980	457	0%	9%	31%	34%	17%	9%
1981	381	0	13	26	31	18	12
1982	376	0	7	30	32	19	12
1983	406	0	11	24	28	19	18
1984	332	0	10	22	31	23	14
1985	321	0%	7%	24%	31%	24%	14%
1986	298	0	7	28	28	21	16
1987	296	1	8	29	23	22	17
1988	339	0	4	25	35	18	18
1989	362	0	10	27	24	22	17
1990	379	1%	7%	26%	23%	21%	22%
1991	359	0	12	29	25	17	17
1992	414	0	12	25	25	16	22
1993	453	1	8	33	24	12	22
1994	459	2	8	25	28	18	19
1995	382	4%	8%	28%	26%	14%	20%
1996	355	0	5	31	23	15	26
1997	361	2	6	28	27	20	18
1998	367	2	7	27	27	22	15

Note: "Total number" includes all instances of justifiable homicide by police, whether or not the age of the police officer is known. The officer's age is known in 70.1% of the justifiable homicides by police between 1976 and 1998.
Due to rounding error, detail may not sum to 100%.
Source: FBI database, *Supplementary Homicide Reports*.

Table 7. Gender and race of police officers who killed felons in justifiable homicides, 1976-98

Year	Total number of justifiable homicides by police	Percent of officers who were —					
		Male			Female		
		White	Black	Other	White	Black	Other
Annual average	373	83%	14%	1%	1%	1%	0%
1976	415	82%	15%	2%	0%	1%	0%
1977	311	82	17	0	1	0	0
1978	313	85	14	0	0	1	0
1979	442	83	15	1	0	1	0
1980	457	85%	13%	0%	1%	1%	0%
1981	381	86	13	0	0	1	0
1982	376	85	14	0	1	0	0
1983	406	89	8	1	1	1	0
1984	332	87	11	2	0	0	0
1985	321	84%	12%	2%	1%	1%	0%
1986	298	89	10	0	1	0	0
1987	296	82	11	2	4	1	0
1988	339	82	12	2	3	1	0
1989	362	84	13	0	3	0	0
1990	379	81%	15%	1%	2%	1%	0%
1991	359	80	17	1	1	1	0
1992	414	81	15	2	1	1	0
1993	453	81	16	1	1	1	0
1994	459	76	22	1	1	0	0
1995	382	83%	14%	1%	1%	1%	0%
1996	355	86	11	1	1	1	0
1997	361	79	16	2	2	1	0
1998	367	80	16	1	2	1	0

Note: "Total number" includes all instances of justifiable homicide by police, whether or not the gender or race of the police officers is known. The officer's gender and race are known in 77.2% of the justifiable homicides by police between 1976 and 1998.
Source: FBI database, *Supplementary Homicide Reports*.

Officers' gender and race

• The officer in a justifiable homicide is almost always a white or black male (97%) (table 7).

• White male officers accounted for 83% of justifiable homicides from 1976 to 1998 and black male officers accounted for 14%.

Officers' and felons' gender

There were 8,578 felons killed by police from 1976 to 1998. In 85% of these homicides the gender of both the felon and the officer was recorded in the national database.

According to FBI national data on justifiable homicides by police from 1976 to 1998 —

• When a justifiable homicide by police occurs, it is almost always a male officer killing a male felon (96%).

• When a male officer kills, the felon killed is almost always a male (98%).

• When a female officer kills, the felon killed is almost always a male (93%).

• When a male felon is killed, the officer is almost always a male (98%).

• When a female felon is killed, the officer is almost always a male (95%).

Officers' and felons' race

In 77% of the 8,578 justifiable homicides by police in the Nation's database, the race of both the felon and the officer was recorded. Some of the justifiable homicides are interracial, with the race of the felon differing from that of the officer. Because statistics on interracial homicide are easily misinterpreted, a few preliminary comments are offered.

If every police officer in the United States were white, then any time a nonwhite person was justifiably killed by police, the homicide would be interracial. This illustrates that the extent to which justifiable homicide is interracial in the United States is influenced by the racial makeup of the police.

Since, according to latest available statistics (1998), approximately 87% of all police officers in the United States are white (11% are black and 2% are of other races), by chance alone the likelihood is high that the officer who kills a nonwhite felon is white. The likelihood is also high that the officer who kills a white felon is white. It should not be surprising to find that most black felons killed by police (just as most white felons killed by police) are killed by a white police officer.

"Chance" factors are not the only ones affecting the likelihood that a justifiable homicide is interracial. Nonchance factors have an effect as well. An obvious one is the policy that police departments may have for assigning officers to particular neighborhoods. A common policy is to assign black officers to black neighborhoods. Consequently, it might be expected that, when a black officer kills a felon, there is a high likelihood that the felon is also black. In line with that expectation, national statistics indicate that most of the felons killed by black officers are themselves black. More generally, national statistics indicate that most justifiable homicides by police are intraracial.

According to FBI national data on justifiable homicides by police from 1976 to 1998 —

• In about 65% of justifiable homicides by police, the officer's race and the felon's race were the same (figure 11).

Intraracial

White officer kills white felon	53.1%
Black officer kills black felon	11.8
Other-race officer kills other-race felon	0.3

Interracial

White officer kills black felon	29.6%
Black officer kills white felon	2.8
White officer kills other-race felon	1.6
Black officer kills other-race felon	0.1
Other-race officer kills white felon	0.5
Other-race officer kills black felon	0.2

• Interracial homicide by police (for example, the killing of a black felon by a white officer or the killing of a white felon by a black officer) make up about a third of justifiable homicides.

Felon statistics give one perspective on the number of police justifiable homicides that are interracial (for example, from 1976 to 1998, police justifiably killed 4,786 white felons, and in 5% of these homicides the officer was black). *Officer* statistics gave another perspective (for example, from 1976 to 1998 white police officers justifiably killed 5,579 felons, and in 35% of these homicides the felon was black). The extent to which justifiable homicide by police officers are interracial depends on which statistics are used:

• When a white officer kills a felon, that felon is usually a white (63%); and when a black officer kills a felon, that felon is usually a black (81%).

• The majority of black felons killed were by white officers (71%); the majority of white felons killed were by white officers (94%); and the majority of other race felons killed were by white officers (81%).

• White-officer-kills-white-felon makes up a growing fraction of all justifiable homicides by police, while white-officer-kills-black-felon makes up a declining fraction (figure 11).

	Percent of all justifiable homicides by police		
	White officer kills —		Black officer kills —
	White felon	Black felon	White felon	Black felon
1978	46%	38%	2%	14%
1988	57	27	3	10
1998	56	24	5	12

Detailed 1998 racial statistics

According to latest statistics (1998) —

• White officers make up 87% of the Nation's 641,208 police and account for 82% of justifiable homicides by police. Black officers make up 11% of the Nation's police and account for 17% of all justifiable homicides.

• White officers (42 justifiable homicides per 100,000 white officers in 1998) and black officers (44 justifiable homicides per 100,000 black officers) commit justifiable homicides at about the same rate, but the rate for officers of other races is lower (25 per 100,000).

• The black-officer-kills-black-felon rate is 32 per 100,000 black officers in 1998, which is higher than the white-officer-kills-black-felon rate of 14 per 100,000 white officers.

• The white-officer-kills-white-felon rate is 28 per 100,000 white officers in 1998, which is higher than the black-officer-kills-white-felon rate of 11 per 100,000 black officers.

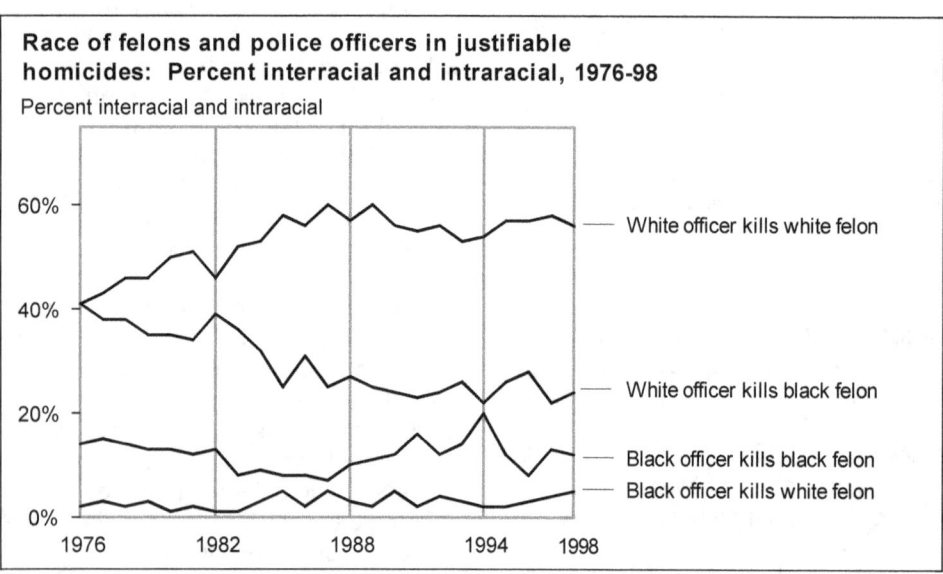

Race of felons and police officers in justifiable homicides: Percent interracial and intraracial, 1976-98

Percent interracial and intraracial

White officer kills white felon
White officer kills black felon
Black officer kills black felon
Black officer kills white felon

Figure 11

The descriptions below are of cases of justifiable homicide by police in 1996. The choice of which cases to describe was left to the police departments that voluntarily prepared and submitted the narratives. Only large urban police departments were asked to participate.

Atlanta

• On Saturday, December 14, 1996, two Atlanta police officers attempted to conduct a traffic stop. The suspect, a 25-year-old male, refused to stop his vehicle and a chase ensued. The suspect wrecked, then exited his vehicle, brandishing a weapon. The officers began to chase the suspect on foot. The suspect then turned and fired several shots in the direction of both officers. One officer returned fire, striking the suspect multiple times. The suspect ran into a nearby apartment complex where he collapsed and died.

• On Thursday, June 6, 1996, at approximately 5:00 p.m., several plain-clothes Atlanta fugitive investigators went to a residence to serve an arrest warrant on a 30-year-old male. The officers approached the residence and identified themselves. The suspect, armed with a loaded handgun, tried to escape through a bedroom window two stories off the ground. When the suspect looked down from the bedroom window, he saw officers outside, on the ground below him. The suspect pointed his weapon in the direction of the officers. One of the officers discharged his service weapon striking the suspect in the chest. The suspect later died at a local hospital.

Baltimore

• At approximately 11:35 a.m., on Monday, June 24, 1996, two uniformed Baltimore City police officers were working as a unit when they observed a large group of individuals in an alley. Knowing the area to be a high-crime, high-drug area, they exited their vehicle to conduct field interviews. At that time, two of the subjects ran from the group.

One officer observed a subject reaching into his waistband, at which time the subject was ordered to the ground by the officer. The other officer observed a second subject reaching into his waistband as he ran from the scene. The suspect removed a dark colored handgun from his waistband. The officers ordered the suspect to drop the weapon, but the suspect refused. The suspect continued to run. Numerous times the officer ordered the suspect to "stop and drop the weapon," but the foot chase continued. The suspect fired several rounds at the officer from his Smith and Wesson .357 caliber revolver. The officer returned fire. The suspect approached a vehicle parked on the road. He entered the vehicle from the passenger side and ordered the operator of the vehicle to "drive!" Instead, the operator fled.

The suspect continued to fire at the officer from the parked vehicle. The officer returned fire, striking the suspect, the vehicle, and two additional vehicles in the immediate area. The suspect was observed slumped in the front passenger seat of the vehicle with a gunshot wound to the right eye and a gunshot wound to the back. He succumbed to his wounds at the scene and was pronounced dead by a medic at 11:48 a.m.

• At approximately 2:15 p.m., on Thursday, January 25, 1996, a Baltimore City police officer was responding to a drug-related call when he was stopped by an elderly male who advised the officer that a male had just discharged a handgun in a nearby park and was still there. The elderly male pointed to the park area and stated, "there he is," as he pointed to a male wearing a black hat, green jacket, and blue jeans standing in the park. The officer broadcast over the police radio information relating to the man armed with a gun, giving both physical and clothing descriptions.

Two plainclothes officers (with visible police ID's on chains around their neck) and one uniformed officer were together in a marked police vehicle when they spotted and approached the suspect.

The suspect was advised by one of the officers to keep his hands in the air where the officers could see them. The suspect turned around to face the officers and lifted up his coat.

The officers could see in the suspect's waistband a black pistol that appeared to be a semi-automatic. The suspect withdrew the pistol and fired at the officers.

The officers returned fire with their departmentally issued weapons (each a Glock model 17). The suspect began to run while continuing to fire at the officers. The officers returned fire until the suspect was incapacitated. When the suspect finally dropped his gun, he was no longer a threat. One officer approached the suspect, kicked the pistol out of the suspect's reach, and handcuffed him.

The officers immediately called for medical personnel because the suspect was still alive. The suspect was uncuffed to receive medical aid. The suspect was pronounced dead of multiple gunshot wounds at a local hospital.

The decedent's green coat was found at the scene with a black ski mask, more than 80 .22 caliber cartridges, and a stainless steel Smith and Wesson break front revolver with 5 .32 caliber cartridges. Less than 1 year prior to his death, the deceased was released from a super maximum security prison where he had served a lengthy sentence for rape and burglary.

• On Thursday, November 7, 1996, at approximately 11:05 a.m., responding to a report of a missing elderly woman, a Baltimore City police officer was sent to investigate the woman's apartment. After discovering the elderly woman stabbed to death on her bed, the officer called the Baltimore City Homicide Unit to assist with a "questionable death" investigation. While searching the apartment for the possible murder weapon, a detective noticed the suspect's feet under a daybed in the living room. The officers ordered the person under the bed to come out. When the suspect did not respond to their commands, the officers began to move the bed, continuing to command the person to get up. Suddenly the suspect jumped up, armed with a large butcher knife raised over his head. The officers demanded several times that the suspect drop the knife, but the suspect refused and began to advance toward one of the officers. Both officers opened fire after the suspect's continued refusal to drop the knife. The suspect fell to the floor after being struck several times in the upper torso. The suspect was a 41-year-old male. He was a drug user with a long prior record of arrests (including rape, assault, and attempted robbery). The elderly woman was his grandmother, with whom he lived. Family of the suspect reported that he frequently stole from her to support his drug habit and had been known to be physically abusive to her, on at least one occasion twisting her arm and pushing her to the ground.

A Baltimore City Fire Department medic responded to the scene and a technician pronounced the suspect dead at 1:22 p.m.

Cleveland

• On Friday, July 26, 1996, at approximately 10:29 p.m., a Cleveland police officer observed a vehicle driving without headlights. When the officer made a traffic stop, the suspect indicated that he had no driver's license. The officer asked the suspect to step out of the car. Rather than obeying, the suspect put the vehicle into reverse, at which time the officer reached into the vehicle in an attempt to turn off the key. The suspect began driving at a high rate of speed holding onto the officer.

The officer was yelling for the suspect to stop the car, but the suspect refused. In response to the officer hitting him with a flashlight, the suspect was

threatening to crash into a pole or a car and "take both of them out." The officer was pleading with the suspect to stop the car. The suspect yelled to the officer, "if we don't hit a pole and kill you, I'm going to pull your gun and shoot you." At that time, the officer checked for his weapon and pulled it out. The officer placed the weapon to the head of the suspect telling him numerous times to stop the vehicle or the officer would be forced to shoot him. When the suspect would not stop, the officer fired one time, striking the suspect in the head. Prior to the vehicle striking a pole, the officer rolled out. The suspect died at the scene.

Houston

• On Sunday, February 18, 1996, a Harris County, Texas, deputy sheriff was working in uniform at an off-duty job in a liquor store. (Officers may work off-duty jobs in uniform after the employer has received a permit from the Harris County Sheriff's Department.) Two males came into the store in an attempt to purchase tequila. The deputy noticed that the males were already intoxicated and advised the clerk not to sell the alcohol. One of the men threw four bottles of mineral water into a tub with other bottles, walked out of the store, and got into his car. Believing the bottles had broken, the deputy attempted to stop the man. The deputy stood between the driver's seat and the open car door, but the suspect refused to turn off his vehicle. As the suspect backed his car away from the liquor store, the deputy was trapped and believed that he would be dragged under the car. Fearing for his life, the deputy fired his weapon two times at the suspect, striking him one time in the chest.

• On Tuesday, February 27, 1996, Houston police officers were searching for a male escapee who was wanted for aggravated assault of a police officer. After receiving a tip on the suspect's location, the officers observed the suspect get off a bus.

As officers approached him, the suspect walked away, then attempted to run. One officer caught the suspect and wrestled him to the ground. As the suspect reached the ground, he pulled a pistol from his pocket and fired at the officers. Officers returned fire, killing the suspect. One sergeant involved in the shooting was shot in the side, but was not seriously injured because he was wearing body armor.

• At approximately 9:57 p.m., on Friday, March 8, 1996, four Houston police officers were dispatched to a "home invasion in progress" call. As the officers approached the house, they observed a male standing in the shadows of the doorway. Officers asked the man to step outside and remove his hands from his pockets. The suspect responded by telling the officers that he had a gun and for the officers to come in and get him. The suspect then ran toward one of the officers, who discharged his weapon at the suspect, severing the left femoral artery.

• On the night of Tuesday, March 12, 1996, a Houston police officer working an off-duty job was called to investigate a loud noise complaint. As the uniformed officer walked from his apartment, he observed two vehicles — one had the engine running. The officer also observed a male standing between the two vehicles. The officer heard a man say, "hurry up," then witnessed the other man jump into the vehicle with its motor running. The officer ordered the occupants to stop. The vehicle struck the officer in the right leg. The officer fired two rounds at the vehicle, but was unsure whether he fired before or after he was struck. Approximately 10 minutes later, one suspect was found dead at his house from a gunshot wound to the head. The other suspect confessed that they were burglarizing a vehicle when the officer confronted them.

• On Thursday, August 8, 1996, Houston police officers were assisting a "neighborhood protection inspector" with inspections of abandoned houses. As officers approached one house, a male walked out of and away from the house. One officer attempted to stop the suspect who was walking away, while the other officer walked onto the porch. When the officer stepped on the porch, another male suspect ran out of the house and grabbed the officer's weapon. Fearing for his life, the officer fired one time, striking the suspect in the chest.

• On Friday, November 8, 1996, at 5:00 a.m., Houston police patrol officers observed two males walking down the street carrying a television, a radio, and a bucket of tools. As officers approached, the suspects began acting suspiciously and speaking Spanish to each other. Officers heard them use the word "pistola." One suspect reached into his pocket as if to retrieve a weapon. In Spanish, the officer ordered the suspect to raise his hands, but the suspect refused. The officer attempted to physically control the suspect, but the suspect broke away and continued reaching into his pocket. Being in fear for his life, the officer fired two times at the suspect. The suspect had been attempting to retrieve an open pocket knife.

• On Tuesday, December 10, 1996, Houston police narcotic officers were attempting to buy 5 kilos of cocaine through an informant. Officers observed four suspects walking into the parking lot with the informant. As one of the officers was parking his car, he heard someone yell, "police, police." The officer then observed one male run past him carrying a gym bag. The officer chased the suspect, identified himself as a police officer, and ordered the man to raise his hands. As the suspect raised his left hand, he pulled a .25 caliber pistol from his right pocket. The officer fired two times at the suspect, striking him in the chest and leg.

• On Sunday, December 15, 1996, a Harris County, Texas, deputy constable was dispatched to a "man down" call. The deputy observed the man lying in the grass and approached him. The man jumped up and grabbed a club, which consisted of two 2x4's nailed together with nails protruding from the wood. The deputy drew his service weapon, but the suspect began advancing toward him and threatening him with the club. After the deputy retreated approximately 140 feet, he shot the suspect one time in the chest.

Los Angeles

• At approximately 6:14 p.m. on Thursday, February 1, 1996, uniformed Los Angeles police officers driving a marked police vehicle approached the subject. The subject produced a 9 mm pistol and fired several shots at the officers, hitting the police vehicle and wounding one officer. Both officers returned fire, wounding the subject. The subject was subsequently transported to a Los Angeles medical center where he expired during surgery.

• At approximately 7:30 p.m. on Saturday, June 22, 1996, Los Angeles police responded to a radio call regarding a "man with a shotgun." Arriving at the scene, officers were confronted by the suspect who was located at the top of a stairwell in front of the apartment door. The suspect was armed with a shotgun.

The Los Angeles Police Department's S.W.A.T. team was notified. S.W.A.T. officers were confronted by the suspect still armed with a shotgun. When the suspect pointed the shotgun at the S.W.A.T. officers, the officers opened fire. The suspect sustained multiple shotgun wounds to his chest.

A Los Angeles Fire Department rescue ambulance responded to the scene, where the suspect was pronounced dead at 11:05 p.m.

• At approximately 6:25 a.m. on Saturday, April 20, 1996, the suspect, armed with a handgun, confronted and threatened to kill several of his apartment complex neighbors. Los Angeles police were notified and responded to the scene.

Upon arrival at the apartment complex, officers were confronted by the suspect, who was still armed with a handgun. The suspect pointed the handgun at several officers, threatening to kill them. An officer-involved shooting occurred and the suspect sustained multiple gunshot wounds.

A Los Angeles City Fire Department rescue ambulance responded to the scene. The suspect was pronounced dead at 7:42 a.m.

• At approximately 9:40 p.m. on Saturday, July 20, 1996, an armed subject confronted Los Angeles police officers. The subject was shot to death.

• At approximately 4:30 p.m. on Sunday, December 22, 1996, two uniformed Los Angeles police officers were investigating a shoplifting in which two six-packs of beer were stolen from a convenience store. As the officers were driving in the alley to the rear of the store, they observed the suspect carrying a six-pack of beer in each hand. As soon as the officers stopped their police vehicle behind the suspect, the suspect turned and immediately walked toward the right side of the police vehicle. The suspect pulled a .380 caliber semiautomatic pistol from his right front pocket and fired two rounds at the officer seated in the front passenger seat. Both officers opened fire with their 9 mm pistols, killing the suspect. As a result of the suspect's gunfire one officer died.

• At approximately 5:00 p.m. on Monday, March 11, 1996, the suspect was driving a vehicle that was stopped in an alley. Uniformed Los Angeles police officers approached the vehicle to conduct a possible stolen vehicle investigation. During the course of the investigation, the suspect started the vehicle in an attempt to flee, dragging the officer alongside.

An officer-involved shooting occurred and the suspect sustained a gunshot wound to his neck. The suspect expired at the scene. Paramedics responded and pronounced the suspect dead at 5:04 p.m.

New York City

• On Monday, April 8, 1996, two New York City police officers were conducting an undercover "buy and bust" drug operation in the Bronx. As one officer approached a group of males to purchase the drugs, he overheard several of the males arguing. During the argument a gun was mentioned. The officer turned back to relay this information to his partner. As the two officers conferred, one officer observed one of the male suspects brandish a gun and fire two bullets at another person in the group. The officers drew their firearms and sought cover behind a telephone pole. One officer identified himself as a police officer and ordered the suspect to drop his weapon. The gunman, standing 25 feet away, turned toward the officers and began firing his 9 mm semi-automatic pistol at them. Both officers returned fire. During the course of the gun battle, the officers exhausted their ammunition supply. The perpetrator, with his gun in hand, then began to advance toward the officers. With no bullets remaining in their pistols, one officer retrieved his off-duty revolver and fired one shot at the advancing gunman, causing him to stagger and collapse to the ground, where he succumbed to his wounds.

• On the morning of Thursday, May 9, 1996, a New York City police officer

was approached by a bus driver who told the officer that he had just seen a man armed with a shotgun enter a crowded office two blocks away. Responding to the location, the officer encountered a detective who had observed several people fleeing the building and had stopped to investigate. Looking through the front window, the officers observed the gunman shouting and waving the shotgun at a female hostage. The officers entered the building and were crawling on their hands and knees toward the rear office when the gunman spotted them and twice fired at them through the office window. As the hostage took cover under a desk, the detective and police officer returned fire, striking the gunman six times and mortally wounding him. A total of 20 hostages were rescued from the location. Recovered from the scene were a 12-gauge shotgun, a fully loaded .22 caliber revolver, 123 rounds, and 103 shotgun shells. It was learned that the gunman had threatened to kill everyone in the office until he located his estranged girlfriend, an employee who had transferred to another office just days earlier.

• Late one Friday night in July 1996, two New York City police officers were on routine patrol when they received a radio broadcast of a "man with a gun." Although they were not yet aware of it, the subject had just robbed a grocery store while armed with a .44 caliber revolver. As they pulled up to the scene, they observed one of the robbery victims running from the store.

He told the officers that the gunman was still inside. Suddenly, the suspect emerged from the store with the weapon in his hand. Despite repeated orders to drop the weapon, the suspect cocked the revolver and aimed it directly at the officers. The officers fired a total of five rounds and mortally wounded the perpetrator.

• On Tuesday, September 3, 1996, two police officers in Staten Island responded to a family dispute.

The officers were met by the complainant across the street from the location. She stated that her estranged husband was in the house, in violation of an order of protection. She said he was not armed and informed the officers that he had ripped the telephone from the wall, forcing her to call the police from outside of the house. As the officers approached the building, the suspect fired a rifle from the second floor of the building, barely missing them, but piercing the gas tanks of a parked vehicle. As the officers took cover, the gunman fired two more shots. Pinned down by the rifle-wielding perpetrator and with no other way to protect either the civilian or themselves, the officers returned fire and mortally wounded the gunman.

Oklahoma City

• At approximately 4:37 p.m. on Thursday, April 4, 1996, Oklahoma City Police Department officers served a warrant for an immediate drug search of a residence. Upon arrival at the residence, the raid officers each went to the position that was assigned during the pre-raid briefing. The front door of the residence was broken open and, before making entry, the officers identified themselves as police officers.

As the first two officers entered the living room, they observed a subject lying on a sofa. The subject raised up and pointed a long barreled handgun at the officers. The two officers fired their service weapons. Both officers stopped shooting when the armed subject collapsed to the floor.

Another subject appeared in the doorway to the living room. He had apparently come from another area of the residence. The officer nearest the doorway was grabbed from behind by the second subject. That officer turned and fired at the second subject. One suspect died at the scene, and the second suspect died later at a local hospital.

• At approximately 12:37 a.m. on Friday, August 6, 1996, several Oklahoma City Police Department officers were attempting to locate an armed subject who was reported to be en route to his girlfriend's residence. Information about the suspect had been announced in a general broadcast over the police radio. The suspect had been recently released from the Oklahoma State penitentiary. Initially, officers did not have an address but after searching phone records from the enhanced 911 system, dispatchers were able to find an address for the subject's girlfriend. While on the phone with someone at the girlfriend's residence, a female dispatcher heard what she thought were three gunshots.

When responding officers arrived at the apartment, the first responding officer knocked on the front door without a response. Officers were able to peer inside the apartment through a window near the front door. From the window the officers observed what appeared to be blood spattered on the walls and a person lying on the floor.

The officers kicked open the apartment's front door. The first officer to enter confirmed a body on the floor. The officer stepped over the body in the hallway and moved toward a bedroom where he observed the body of another female also on the floor. A small child was sitting on the shoulder of the dead female, looking at the officer. Another child was nearby. As the officer began to move into the bedroom, a voice from the bedroom warned the officer that if he came in he would be shot. The only light in the bedroom was that of a television. The officer observed the silhouette of a man holding a handgun. The officer immediately retreated to a nearby bathroom. The officers identified themselves and ordered the suspect to drop his weapon. When the gunman changed locations inside the bedroom, the officer attempted to verbally coax the children out of the bedroom.

From inside the bedroom and out of sight of the officer, the suspect announced he was going to push the two children out through the bedroom door. As the suspect came into view of the officer in the bathroom, the officer could see that the suspect was still armed with a handgun. The suspect moved and was standing directly over the body of the dead female. He began to raise his weapon and then pointed it in the direction of the officer in the bedroom. The officer responded by firing two rounds from his .45 caliber service weapon. Both rounds struck the suspect, killing him. The deceased suspect had just committed three homicides.

• At approximately 5:25 a.m. on Tuesday, November 16, 1996, several Oklahoma City Police Department officers met for breakfast at a local 24-hour restaurant. While adjusting tables to accommodate other officers who had not yet arrived, the officers observed a subject sitting in a booth by himself. The subject matched the description of a suspect who was wanted in connection with an "assault with a deadly weapon with intent to kill" that had occurred earlier in the evening.

One officer went over to the suspect while the other officers moved into position to back up the confronting officer. To confirm that the suspect was the one who was wanted for the assault, the officer asked to look at the suspect's forearm. The officer was looking for an identifying tattoo.

When the officer saw the identifying tattoo, he immediately began to back away from the booth where the suspect was seated. The seated suspect, with his right hand, reached into his waistband and produced a semiautomatic pistol. The officer ordered the suspect down, but the suspect ignored the order and brought the gun above the table top. All four officers began shooting at the suspect. The suspect was struck several times and died at the scene.

Philadelphia

• On Friday, June 21, 1996, at approximately 3:38 p.m., a Philadelphia police officer responded to a "man with a knife" disturbance. Upon arrival at the residence, the officer was informed by a woman yelling from the second floor of the house that the suspect was downstairs in the house. She told the officer to enter through the front door as it was already open. The officer drew his gun, then entered the residence. Inside, a 50-year-old male was carrying a steak knife while walking out of the kitchen and toward the officer. Despite several demands from the officer to drop the knife, the suspect continued to approach the officer. The officer fired his service weapon (a Glock model 17) one time striking the suspect in the chest. With the knife still in his right hand, the suspect fell to the floor. When rescue services and back-up officers arrived, the knife was recovered and the suspect was transported to a local hospital. The suspect was pronounced dead at 4:05 p.m.

• On Friday, November 15, 1996, at approximately 8:51 a.m., a Philadelphia police officer at a school crossing was approached by a 29-year-old male in a car. The man asked for directions. The officer noticed a gun in the suspect's vehicle. While the officer was investigating the incident, the suspect pulled out another gun and shot at the officer, striking him one time in the chest. The officer returned fire, striking the suspect several times in the chest and neck. Both officer and suspect were taken to a local hospital. Because the officer had been wearing a bullet-proof vest, he was not seriously injured and was soon released. The suspect was pronounced dead at 9:20 a.m.

• On Sunday, November 17, 1996, at approximately 1:08 a.m., three Philadelphia police officers responded to a "burglary in progress" call. While covering the rear of the residence, two officers witnessed a male exiting the property. The suspect fired a weapon at the officers. Both officers returned fire with their service weapons (Glock, model 17; Glock, model 19), hitting the suspect in the chest, neck, shoulder, and hand.

A second male suspect pushed open the front door. Seeing a police officer covering the front of the residence, the second suspect fired a weapon from inside the house at the officer. The officer returned fire, hitting the second suspect in the chest. The suspect collapsed on the sidewalk in front of the house. At the time of the shooting, the other two officers were inside the house.

The first suspect was taken to a local hospital where he was pronounced dead. The second suspect was pronounced dead at the scene. Both guns used by the suspects were recovered at the scene.

Police officers murdered by felons, 1976-98

Throughout this report, the term "police officer" refers to persons with sworn arrest powers. Such persons include sheriffs, deputies, State troopers, and other law enforcement officers.

When a felon murders a police officer in the line of duty, the deceased officer's agency voluntarily sends a record of the offense to the FBI in Washington. The record is then entered into a national database. The database contains such information as the officer's age, race, and gender, the number of years as a police officer, and such information on the felon as age, race, gender, and prior record.

Drop in murders of police officers

According to national data on felonious killings of police officers —

• 1,820 law enforcement officers were murdered between 1976 and 1998.

• On average, 79 law enforcement officers were murdered in the United States each year from 1976 to 1998, but the annual number is dropping (figure 12).

	Number of police officers murdered
1978	93
1988	78
1998	61

• There is little correspondence between trends in the murder of police officers and trends in justifiable homicides by police (the correlation is +0.3) (figure 13).

• Of all the murders of police officers from 1987 to 1998 (834), about 1 in 6, or 15% (129), were by felons who were then killed by police in a justifiable homicide.

• Of all the justifiable homicides by police from 1987 to 1998 (4,535), about 3% (129) were of felons who had murdered a police officer.

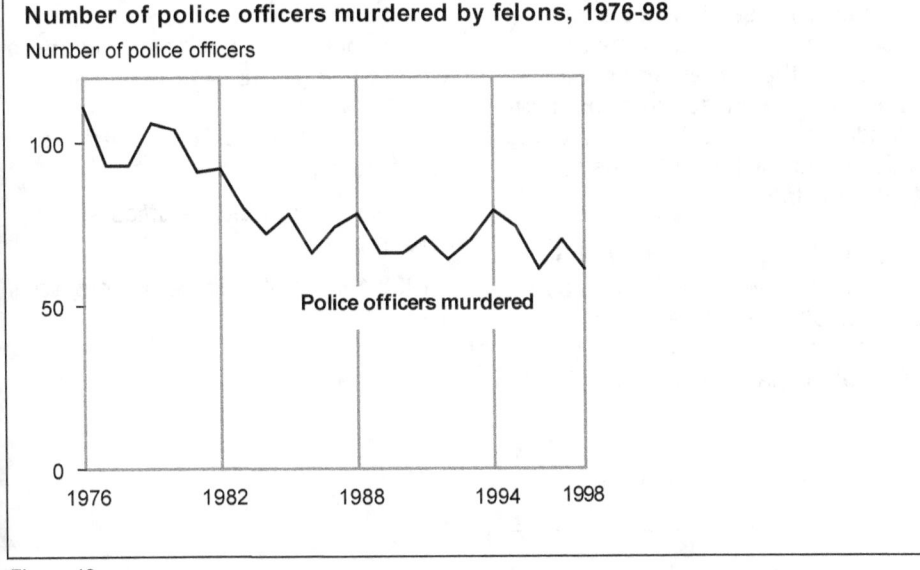

Number of police officers murdered by felons, 1976-98

Number of police officers

Police officers murdered

Figure 12

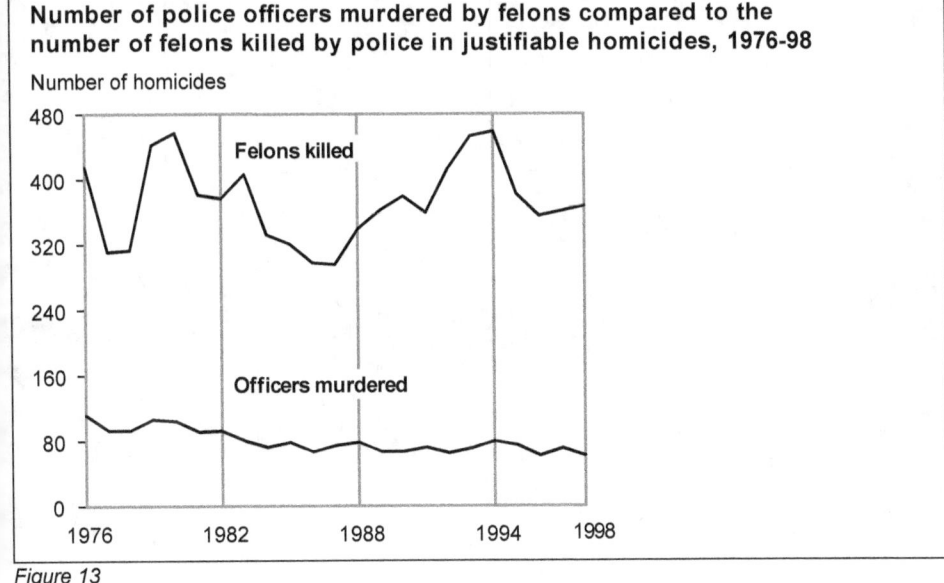

Number of police officers murdered by felons compared to the number of felons killed by police in justifiable homicides, 1976-98

Number of homicides

Felons killed

Officers murdered

Figure 13

Table 8. Police officers murdered by felons: Percent wearing body armor at the time of death, 1981-98	
Year	Percent of murdered officers wearing body armor
Annual average	33%
1981	12%
1982	15
1983	25
1984	24
1985	19%
1986	24
1987	25
1988	26
1989	32
1990	25%
1991	34
1992	27
1993	56
1994	47
1995	46%
1996	56
1997	42
1998	57

Note: Data on police killed wearing body armor are not available prior to 1981.
Source: FBI, *Law Enforcement Officers Killed and Assaulted*.

Perhaps an explanation for the drop in police officer murders has something to do with increasing police use of bullet-proof vests and other types of body armor. Presumably the more often that police wear body armor, the less often that police die in violent encounters with felons. Needed to test this explanation are annual statistics that indicate what percentage of law enforcement officers wear body armor. While such statistics apparently do not exist, annual statistics do exist that indicate what percentage of murdered officers are wearing armor at the time of their attack. These statistics should suffice so long as it is assumed that increases in the percentage of murdered officers wearing armor mirror a broader trend toward increasing use of body armor by police. Consistent with this explanation —

• Police wearing of body armor has risen (as reflected in the percentage of murdered officers who are wearing armor at the time of their attack) and police deaths have fallen (table 8).

Other factors beyond increased use of body armor probably have contributed to the drop in murders of police officers. These other factors include better training, better communications, and better police practices.

Drop in rate of murder of police officers

From 1976 to 1998, on average 17 of every 100,000 police officers were murdered annually. Each year this was an average of more than 1 murdered for every 6,500 law enforcement officers.

A police officer's risk of being murdered has dropped (figure 14):

In 1978, 1 in 4,000 police officers was murdered

In 1988 1 in 6,000 police officers was murdered

In 1998 1 in 11,000 police officers was murdered.

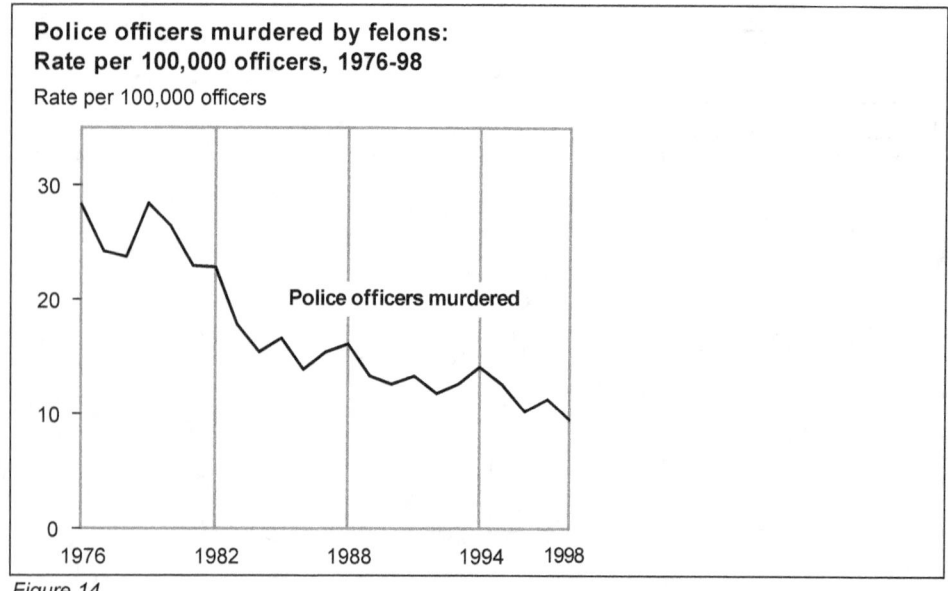

Police officers murdered by felons: Rate per 100,000 officers, 1976-98

Rate per 100,000 officers

Police officers murdered

Figure 14

Table 9. Police officers murdered by felons: Percent killed with firearm and percent slain with own weapon, 1976-98

Year	Total number of officers murdered	Percent of murdered police officers killed with —	
		a firearm	their own firearm
Annual average	79	92%	12%
1976	111	85%	14%
1977	93	89	10
1978	93	98	15
1979	106	94	16
1980	104	91%	13%
1981	91	95	13
1982	92	89	5
1983	80	93	15
1984	72	92	17
1985	78	90%	14%
1986	66	94	23
1987	74	89	18
1988	78	97	15
1989	66	86	15
1990	66	86%	5%
1991	71	96	11
1992	64	86	6
1993	70	96	7
1994	79	99	8
1995	74	84%	8%
1996	61	93	7
1997	70	96	7
1998	61	95	10

Source: FBI, *Law Enforcement Officers Killed and Assaulted.*

Police officers murdered with their own firearm

Firearms claimed the lives of 92% of the 1,820 law enforcement officers murdered from 1976 to 1998 (table 9).

Twelve percent of murdered officers were killed with their own firearms during the 23-year period. The vast majority of the officers who were slain with their own weapons were killed with a handgun.

Police officers slain with their own firearm

	Number	Percent
1978	14	15.1%
1988	12	15.0
1998	6	9.8

Circumstances at scene of incident

On average, 39% of officers lost their lives during arrest situations. One in six officers (16%) were killed while responding to disturbance calls, 14% were killed while enforcing traffic laws, 14% were slain while investigating suspicious persons or circumstances, and 11% were killed in an ambush situation (table 10).

Table 10. Police officers murdered by felons: Circumstances at scene of incident, 1976-98

Year	Total number of officers murdered	Disturbance calls	Arrest situations	Civil disorders	Handling, transporting, custody of prisoners	Investigating suspicious persons/ circumstances	Ambush situation	Mentally deranged	Traffic pursuits/ stops
Annual average	79	16%	39%	0%	4%	14%	11%	2%	14%
1976	111	18%	44%	0%	4%	10%	12%	4%	9%
1977	93	24	42	0	8	10	4	0	13
1978	93	11	42	0	8	9	13	3	15
1979	106	16	44	0	3	9	10	4	14
1980	104	12%	46%	0%	1%	16%	7%	2%	16%
1981	91	21	41	0	1	11	10	2	14
1982	92	20	39	1	3	11	10	2	14
1983	80	19	39	0	4	13	11	1	14
1984	72	11	49	0	4	14	11	0	11
1985	78	17%	37%	0%	5%	12%	9%	0%	21%
1986	66	9	39	0	8	17	8	5	15
1987	74	30	37	0	8	7	6	1	11
1988	78	9	42	0	3	28	9	1	8
1989	66	20	36	0	9	15	6	3	11
1990	66	15%	46%	0%	3%	14%	12%	2%	9%
1991	71	24	20	0	9	14	16	0	18
1992	64	17	42	0	3	11	11	0	16
1993	70	14	40	0	1	21	7	1	14
1994	79	10	42	0	1	19	10	5	13
1995	74	11%	28%	0%	5%	23%	19%	1%	12%
1996	61	7	41	0	0	21	12	2	18
1997	70	20	30	0	6	14	17	1	11
1998	61	26	26	0	7	10	16	0	15

Note: Detail may not sum to 100% due to rounding error. Disturbance calls include: bar fights, man with gun, family quarrels. Arrests situations include: burglaries in progress/pursuing burglary suspects, robberies in progress/pursuing robbery suspects, drug-related matters, attempting other arrests. Civil disorders include: mass disobedience, riot. Ambush situations include: entrapment/premeditation, unprovoked attack.
Source: FBI, *Law Enforcement Officers Killed and Assaulted.*

Murdered police officers

According to FBI national data on felonious killings of police officers from 1976 to 1998 —

Officers' age

• 65% were over 30 years of age (table 11).

Officer's age
Under 25	8%
25 to 30	27
31 to 40	36
41 or older	29

Officers' gender

• Police officers slain in the line of duty were almost always males (98%) (table 12).

Table 11. Age of police officers murdered by felons, 1976-98

Year	Percent of murdered officers who were —			
	Under 25	25-30	31-40	41 or older
Annual average	8%	27%	36%	29%
1976	11%	32%	28%	29%
1977	11	39	23	27
1978	14	30	30	26
1979	9	20	41	30
1980	12%	26%	43%	19%
1981	13	23	42	22
1982	9	24	44	23
1983	10	30	45	15
1984	6	28	40	26
1985	5%	26%	35%	34%
1986	8	30	29	33
1987	11	26	32	31
1988	15	15	40	30
1989	5	20	38	37
1990	5%	14%	41%	40%
1991	7	27	36	30
1992	6	21	39	34
1993	6	38	34	22
1994	8	26	38	28
1995	8%	26%	24%	42%
1996	4	35	39	22
1997	2	26	35	37
1998	11	30	28	31

Source: FBI, *Law Enforcement Officers Killed and Assaulted.*

Table 12. Gender of police officers murdered by felons, 1976-98

Year	Percent of murdered officers	
	Male	Female
Annual average	98%	2%
1976	100%	0%
1977	99	1
1978	100	0
1979	99	1
1980	99%	1%
1981	98	2
1982	97	3
1983	100	0
1984	94	6
1985	96%	4%
1986	98	2
1987	100	0
1988	97	3
1989	97	3
1990	98%	2%
1991	96	4
1992	100	0
1993	94	6
1994	96	4
1995	99%	1%
1996	96	4
1997	100	0
1998	90	10

Source: FBI, *Law Enforcement Officers Killed and Assaulted.*

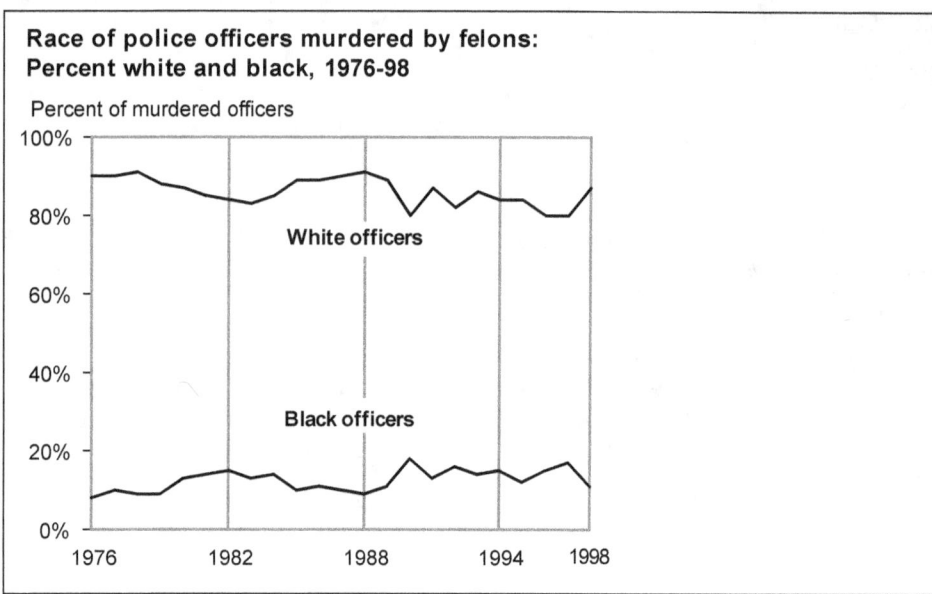

Race of police officers murdered by felons: Percent white and black, 1976-98

Percent of murdered officers

- White officers
- Black officers

Figure 15

Table 13. Police officers murdered by felons: Percent wearing uniform at time of death, 1976-98

Year	Percent wearing uniform
Annual average	72%
1976	71%
1977	81
1978	80
1979	71
1980	69%
1981	80
1982	52
1983	80
1984	75
1985	73%
1986	67
1987	79
1988	68
1989	67
1990	63%
1991	73
1992	65
1993	81
1994	63
1995	66%
1996	78
1997	75
1998	79

Source: FBI, *Law Enforcement Officers Killed and Assaulted.*

Table 14. Age of felons who murdered police officers: Percent under age 18 and age 18-30, 1976-98

	Percent of murderers of police officers who were —	
Year	Under age 18	Age 18-30
Annual average	10%	54%
1976	10%	45%
1977	11	58
1978	8	62
1979	5	60
1980	9%	62%
1981	7	46
1982	5	57
1983	8	47
1984	20	53
1985	4%	59%
1986	2	58
1987	13	41
1988	5	63
1989	7	42
1990	8%	53%
1991	9	60
1992	13	54
1993	20	47
1994	18	47
1995	18%	46%
1996	7	66
1997	3	58
1998	13	58

Source: FBI, *Law Enforcement Officers Killed and Assaulted.*

Officers' race

• 86% of murdered officers were white and 13% were black (figure 15).

Officers' other characteristics

• 72% of officers murdered from 1976 to 1996 were wearing their uniform (table 13).

• Murdered police officers had an average of 9 years of law enforcement service.

Years of service
Less than 1	6%
1 to 4	29
5 to 10	31
Over 10	34

Detailed racial statistics for the 1990's

• According to statistics for 1993-98, white police officers made up about 87% of all police officers in the United States and 83% of all police officers murdered by felons. Black officers were 11% of police officers but 15% of those murdered, and officers of other races were 2% of police officers and 2% of those murdered.

Felons who murdered police officers

According to FBI national data on felonious killings of police officers from 1976 to 1998 —

Felons' age

• Most persons who murdered police were ages 18 to 30 (54%) (table 14).

According to FBI national data on felonious killings of police officers from 1976 to 1998 —

Felons' gender

• Persons who murdered a police officer were almost always males (97%) (table 15).

Felons' race

• Most persons who murdered a police officer were white (54%) (table 16).

• Blacks made up about 12% of the U.S. population but were 43% of the felons who murdered a police officer; whites were about 83% of the U.S. population but about 54% of murderers of police officers.

• Murderers of police officers represent a tiny fraction of the total population. Of the Nation's 89 million white males (age 13 or older), 35 murdered a police officer in 1998. Of the 12 million black males (age 13 or older), 21 murdered an officer that year. White males were 41% of the U.S. population (age 13 or older) and 58% of those who murdered a law enforcement officer. Black males were 6% of the population (age 13 or older) and 35% of the murderers of officers.

Table 15. Gender of felons who murdered police officers, 1976-98

| Year | Percent of murderers of police officers | |
	Male	Female
Annual average	97%	3%
1976	94%	6%
1977	99	1
1978	94	6
1979	97	3
1980	93%	7%
1981	96	4
1982	95	5
1983	97	3
1984	98	2
1985	99%	1%
1986	97	3
1987	91	9
1988	98	2
1989	96	4
1990	94%	6%
1991	99	1
1992	99	1
1993	99	1
1994	96	4
1995	92%	8%
1996	99	1
1997	100	0
1998	99	1

Source: FBI, *Law Enforcement Officers Killed and Assaulted.*

Table 16. Race of felons who murdered police officers, 1976-98

| Year | Percent of murderers of police officers | | |
	White	Black	Other
Annual average	54%	43%	3%
1976	54%	43%	3%
1977	58	37	5
1978	56	39	5
1979	51	47	2
1980	57%	43%	0%
1981	41	57	2
1982	61	38	1
1983	66	32	2
1984	55	38	7
1985	47%	50%	3%
1986	60	37	3
1987	65	35	0
1988	58	42	0
1989	56	42	2
1990	56%	43%	1%
1991	54	45	1
1992	53	46	1
1993	43	57	0
1994	54	43	3
1995	56%	40%	4%
1996	45	48	7
1997	50	41	9
1998	58	35	7

Source: FBI, *Law Enforcement Officers Killed and Assaulted.*

According to FBI national data on felonious killings of police officers from 1976 to 1998 —

Felons' criminal record

• Two-thirds of the felons who murdered a police officer had a prior criminal arrest (figure 16).

• Half were convicted in the past.

• A third had a prior arrest for a violent crime.

• A fifth were on parole or on probation at the time of the murder.

• 4% had a prior arrest for murder charges.

• 24% had a prior arrest for narcotic drug law violations.

• 11% had a prior arrest for assaulting police or resisting arrest.

• 28% had a prior arrest for weapons violations.

Felons' race and officers' race, 1980-98

A total of 1,417 law enforcement officers were murdered during the period 1980 to 1998, and —

• In most of the murders of police officers between 1980 and 1998 (62%), the officer's race and the felon's race were the same:

Intraracial
White felon kills white officer	51.9%
Black felon kills black officer	10.0
Other-race felon kills other-race officer	0.6

Interracial
White felon kills black officer	2.4%
Black felon kills white officer	28.5
White felon kills other-race officer	0.4
Black felon kills other-race officer	0.0
Other-race felon kills white officer	2.6
Other-race felon kills black officer	0.1
Multiple felons of different races kill —	
white officer	2.9%
black officer	0.6
other-race officer	0.0

• 38% of murders of police officers are interracial (for example, a white felon killing a black officer, or a black felon killing a white officer).

Victim statistics provide one perspective on the number of police murders that are interracial (for example, of all black officers murdered from 1980 to 1998, 19% were murdered by a white felon). *Offender* statistics provide another perspective (for example, of all white felons who murdered a police officer from 1980 to 1998, 3% of the murdered officers were black).

The extent to which murders of police officers are interracial depends on which statistics — victim or offender — are used:

• When a white police officer is murdered, the offender is usually a white (60%); and when a black police officer is murdered, the offender is usually a black (76%).

• When a black felon murders a police officer, the officer is usually a white (74%); and when a white felon murders a police officer, the officer is usually a white (95%).

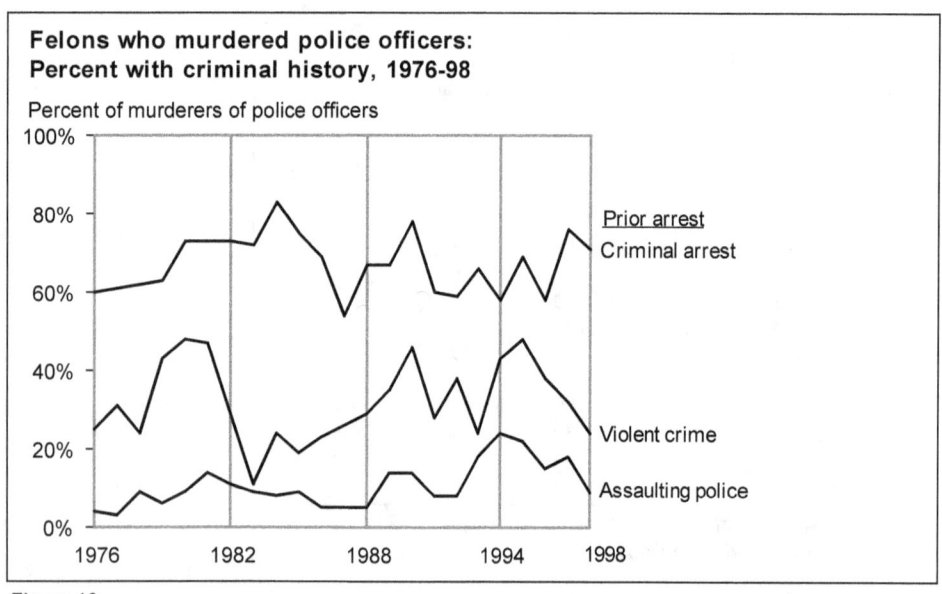

Felons who murdered police officers: Percent with criminal history, 1976-98

Figure 16

Felons' age, race, and gender, 1980-98

• Murderers of police officers represent a tiny fraction of the total population. Of the Nation's 18.3 million young white males (white males ages 13 to 24), 17 murdered a police officer in 1998. Of the 3.4 million young black males, 13 murdered an officer that year.

On average from 1980 to 1998 —

• Young white males made up about 8% of the population but 20% of felons who murdered a police officer (figure 17). Young black males made up about 1% of the population but 21% of felons who murdered a police officer.

• Young black males murdered police officers at a rate almost 6 times that of young white males (5.7 versus 1 per million population) (figure 18).

Descriptions of actual cases of police officers killed in the line of duty

Descriptions of actual cases of police officers killed in the line of duty can be found in the annual FBI publication, *Law Enforcement Officers Killed and Assaulted*, or on the FBI website at http://www.fbi.gov/ucr.htm.

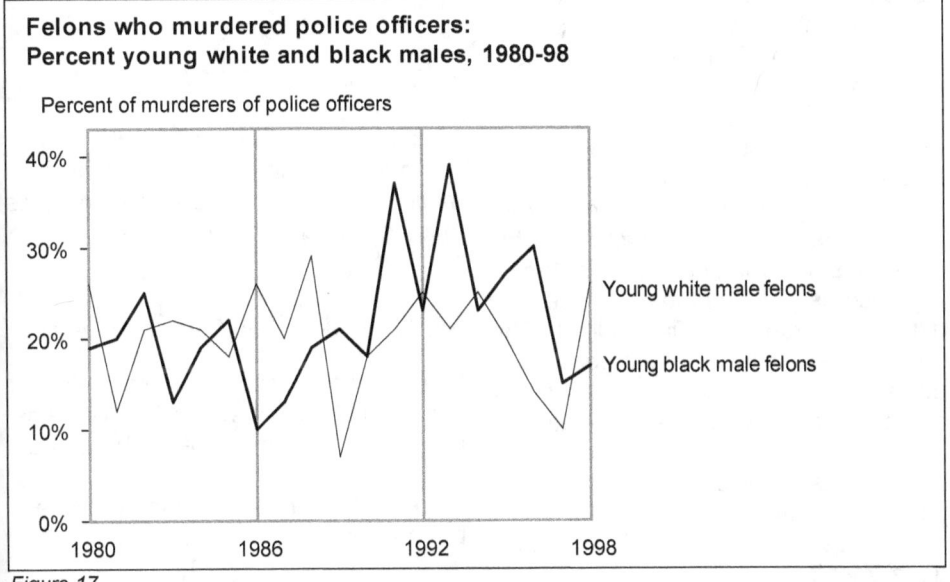

Felons who murdered police officers: Percent young white and black males, 1980-98

Percent of murderers of police officers

Figure 17

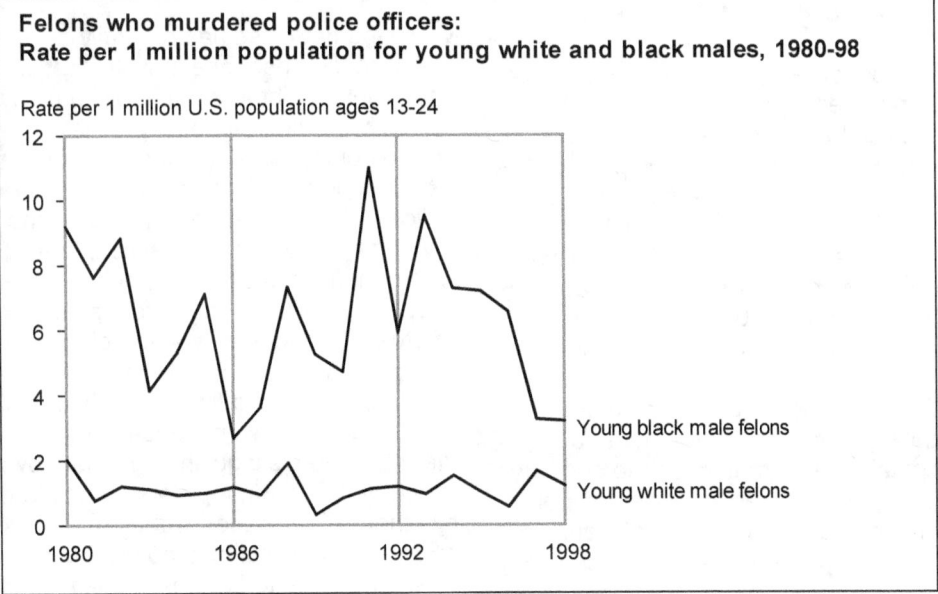

Felons who murdered police officers: Rate per 1 million population for young white and black males, 1980-98

Rate per 1 million U.S. population ages 13-24

Figure 18

Methodology

The SHR national database on justifiable homicides by police

Ideally, every time police kill a felon in a justifiable homicide, a record of the event is sent to the FBI in Washington. Each record of justifiable homicide received by the FBI is then entered into the Supplemental Homicide Reports (SHR) database.

The number of justifiable homicides by police in the year is available in two places: the SHR database and the FBI annual publication *Crime in the United States*. (The first published count covers 1987.)

Published counts found in *Crime in the United States* do not agree precisely with the number of justifiable homicides by police found in the database (see below). Moreover, in certain years there are police justifiable homicides in a State that are unaccounted for either in the annual publication or in the SHR database. (The FBI publication routinely summarizes year-to-year counts of justifiable homicides in a table. Summary counts in this table are often not national in scope. To avoid confusion, the table should alert readers when States are missing.)

Two sources of FBI statistics on the annual number of justifiable homicides by police: published versus SHR database

Year	Published	SHR	Difference
1998	365	367	2
1997	366	361	5
1996	358	355	3
1995	389	382	7
1994	462	459	3
1993	455	453	2
1992	418	414	4
1991	366	359	7
1990	385	379	6
1989	363	362	1
1988	343	339	4
1987	300	296	4

Evolution of the SHR database

Three stages describe the evolution of the SHR database.

1. *Early stage: 1963 to 1967*

In the early 1960's the FBI started the SHR database. Police departments across the Nation began sending to the FBI a record of each murder (including nonnegligent manslaughter) in their jurisdiction. The first records covered murders occurring in 1963.

The FBI decided to expand the database to include justifiable homicides by police and civilians. The first records received were for justifiable homicides occurring in 1966 and 1967. The records included the age, race, and gender of persons justifiably killed. The age, gender, and race of the police officers involved in the homicides were not included because this information was not requested. The FBI did not disseminate statistics on 1966 and 1967 justifiable homicides because the records were based on too few police departments.

2. *Middle stage: 1968 to 1975*

The cooperation of the Nation's police departments grew to the point where the FBI began disseminating statistics on justifiable homicides by police. The earliest statistics covered those justifiable homicides occurring in 1968. Statistics from 1968 to 1986 were not published but were made available upon request. FBI statistics from 1987 and later were routinely published.

Justifiable homicides in the SHR database for 1968 through 1975 contained information on the age, race, and gender of persons killed by police, but no information on the officers involved in these incidents. According

to the database, the number of justifiable homicides by police from 1968 to 1975 was:

Year	Number of justifiable homicides by police
1968	395
1969	424
1970	412
1971	557
1972	469
1973	492
1974	553
1975	559

3. *Current stage: 1976 to present*

After 1975 the FBI expanded the scope of the SHR database to include information (age, race, gender) on the police officers who commit justifiable homicide.

Nonjustifiable homicide by police

In addition to justifiable homicides by police, the SHR database also contains records of two other types of homicide:

• a record of each justifiable homicide by citizens

• a record of each murder.

While the database has primarily a statistical purpose, one statistic that is impossible to obtain from it (or from any currently existing database) is the number of murders by police. Murder is a type of nonjustifiable homicide. If a police officer deliberately kills someone and the homicide is not justified, that type of nonjustifiable homicide is supposed to go into the database as a "murder." Undoubtedly some of the "murders" in the SHR database are murders by police officers, but their number is unknown because nothing in the database distinguishes murders by police officers from murders committed by others. Consequently the annual number of nonjustifiable homicides by police in the United States is unknown.

Errors in the SHR database

Justifiable homicides by police for an entire State are sometimes missing from the SHR database. One way of determining whether a State is missing in a particular year is to examine the number of justifiable homicides that State reported in previous years. If the State reports a sizable number year after year but then reports none, that probably indicates the State is missing from the database. For example, in a large State such a Florida, there is at least one justifiable homicide by police each year. Yet none are recorded in the SHR database for Florida for certain years.

The opposite problem — too many rather than too few records of justifiable homicide by police in the database — also exists. To understand how that happens, imagine an officer deliberately killing a citizen in circumstances that initially appear to warrant lethal force. The police department sends a record to the FBI showing the incident to be a justifiable homicide, but some time later a judge or jury decides that the killing was unlawful and finds the officer guilty of murder. The FBI urges police departments to send in a revised record in such situations so that the SHR database can be updated. But if the police department fails to do that, the killing will remain in the database as a "justifiable homicide by police" when it should instead be coded as a "murder" on the "circumstance" variable.

Nonjustifiable homicides by police in the SHR database

The number of nonjustifiable homicides by police (or murders) incorrectly labeled as "justifiable homicide" in the SHR database is unknown. One way to spot these errors is to find in the database a case labeled as "justifiable homicide by police" that actually involved a police officer known to have been convicted of murder for that homicide.

If the SHR database had the name of the officer who committed the homicide, the process would be fairly simple: find the officer's name and check to see if the homicide is classified as "justifiable homicide by police" or "murder." But the database has no names. So the check must rely on other recorded information about the incident: the month and year of the homicide; the police agency in whose jurisdiction the homicide occurred; the age, race, and gender of the victim; the age, race, and gender of the offender; the type of weapon used; the number of victims in the incident; the number of offenders in the incident; and victim-offender relationship.

To illustrate this type of check, eight news accounts were obtained of police officers convicted of murder in the line of duty. In four of the eight the check was inconclusive:

1. The SHR database has a record of a homicide occurring in the place and on the date shown in the news account, but the database is missing too much data to match the news account.

2. The SHR database has a record of a homicide occurring in the place and on the date shown in the news account, but some of the information in the SHR database does not match the homicide in the news account.

For the remaining four news accounts the homicide characteristics in the SHR database did match those in the news account.

1. In two cases the homicide is classified correctly as "murder." In both cases there is evidence of an update, possibly to change the classification from "justifiable homicide by police" to "murder" when the officer was convicted.

2. The other two cases are coded incorrectly: one as "justifiable homicide by police" and one as "undetermined."

The news accounts indicated that the police officers involved in these two cases were convicted of murder or manslaughter.

Justifiable homicides by police missing from the SHR database

The number of missing justifiable homicides by police is unknown, but one way to spot missing records is by examining reporting by States that, because of their large populations, are almost certain to have had at least one justifiable homicide by police in a year. A year with no recorded justifiable homicide by police suggests missing information. A problem with this method of identifying missing data is that a State can still have a sizable number of justifiable homicides in the database even when a big city police department in that State fails to send in any records. Nevertheless, it is instructive to search the SHR database for years in which a large State has no justifiable homicides. For 1976 to 1998, the results are summarized below:

Year	States with justifiable homicides by police but no record of them in the SHR database that year
1988	Florida, Kentucky
1989	Florida
1990	Florida
1991	Florida
1993	Kansas
1994	Kansas
1995	Illinois, Kansas
1996	District of Columbia, Kansas
1997	Florida, Kansas
1998	District of Columbia, Florida, Kansas, and Wisconsin

Statistics given in this report were not adjusted to account for missing States. For example, figure 1 "national" counts of justifiable homicides are not adjusted for justifiable homicides thought to be missing for two States (Florida and Kentucky) in 1988. However, were adjustment made by including in the figure only those States that were missing no data throughout the period from 1976 to 1998, figure 1 would not look much different from how it looks now.

Adjusted and unadjusted numbers of justifiable homicides by police have a strong positive correlation (+0.95).

Similarly, figure 2 "national" rates of justifiable homicide are not adjusted for States missing for certain years. To illustrate, no justifiable homicides were recorded for Kansas 1995, but the base for the 1995 "national" rate includes the Kansas population. However, excluding populations of missing States would have made little difference since adjusted and unadjusted rates of justifiable homicides by police have a strong positive correlation (+0.99).

Misinformation in the SHR database regarding officer characteristics

Of the 8,578 records in the SHR database on justifiable homicides by police from 1976 to 1998, about 5,800 records include both the felon's and the officer's age, race, and gender. In about 4.6% of these 5,800 records (270 cases), the felon's and officer's age, race, and gender are identical. For example, the SHR database describes both the felon and the officer as a 41-year-old white male.

By chance alone the age, race, and gender of the felon and the officer can be the same, but a 4.6% match rate is too high to be explained solely by chance. (The likelihood of a chance match is no more than 1% of cases.)

One explanation for identical felon and officer characteristics may be confusion about how to fill out the FBI form. The form for reporting justifiable homicide is the same one used to report murders. The form designates the person who commits the murder as the "offender" and the murdered person as the "victim." Police agencies reporting a justifiable homicide by police are instructed to record the felon's age, race, and gender under "victim's age," "victim's race," and "victim's gender." The officer's age, race, and gender are to be recorded under "offender's age," "offender's race," and "offender's

gender." To police agencies, the only "offenders" in a justifiable homicide are the felons. Consequently, police agencies may occasionally report felon characteristics under both "victim" and "offender" headings.

The effect of such occasional errors on the national statistics presented in this report is generally small. Excluding cases in which the age, race, and gender of felon and officer are identical made little difference in this report's main findings. The one instance of a sizable effect was the percentage of all justifiable homicides that were "black officer kills black felon" (figure 11). The percent of justifiable homicide that were "black officer kills black felon" was 14% in 1993, 20% in 1994, and 12% in 1995. The large rise from 14% in 1993 to 20% in 1994 was due to a large number of justifiable homicides in 1994 that involved felons and officers with identical characteristics. More specifically, the large increase is attributable to the New York City Police Department's reporting an unusually large number of "black officer kills black felon" justifiable homicides.

Over the 23 years from 1976 to 1998, 270 felons killed in justifiable homicides had the same age, race, and gender as the officer. Of the 270 felons, 68.9% were white, 30.7% were black, and .4% were of other races.

Missing characteristics of felons and officers in the SHR database

The gender, race, and age of felons killed by police are rarely missing in the SHR database (data for figure 8). However, it is not uncommon for the gender, race, and age of the officers to be missing.

Cautionary note on this report's statistics on justifiable homicides by police

All statistics in this report on justifiable homicides by police are known to be missing homicides by police in Florida from 1988 to 1991, 1997, and 1998; in Kentucky in 1988; in Kansas from 1993 to 1998; in Illinois in 1995; Wisconsin in 1998; and in the District of Columbia in 1996 and 1998. Other justifiable homicides by police are probably missing as well. In addition, some small but unknown number of homicides labeled "justifiable homicides by police" are probably nonjustifiable homicides.

Certain statistics (for example, the number and rate of justifiable homicides by police) are probably more affected by these errors than other statistics in the report (for example, the percentage of persons killed who are male, and the percentage of justifiable homicides that involve a firearm).

Justifiable homicides by police in cases involving more than one officer

In 86% of justifiable homicides by police, there was a single police officer ("1-officer cases"), in 10% there were 2 officers ("2-officer cases"), and in the remaining 4% there were 3 or more. In this report's tabulations, when more than one officer killed the felon, the officer described first in the database supplied the officer's characteristics (age, race, and gender). Using just the characteristics of the first officer is sensible if that officer resembles the other officers in the incident. To check the resemblance, first-officer and second-officer characteristics were compared, and results indicated that, in the vast majority of cases, there was a close match.

Source of national statistics on police officers murdered by felons

Most of the data in this report on murdered police officers were obtained directly from the annual FBI publication *Law Enforcement Officers Killed or Assaulted*. However, the source of the 1980-98 data on interracial and intraracial murder of police officers was a tabulation prepared by the FBI specifically for this report.

Source of size and characteristics of U.S. police force

The source for the number of full-time sworn officers in the Nation is the FBI's annual publication *Crime in the United States*. Regarding the racial make-up of the Nation's police officers in the 1990's, the only existing data are for 1993 and 1997. The BJS publications containing the 1993 data are:

• *Local Police Departments, 1993*, April 1996, NCJ 148822.

• *Sheriffs' Departments, 1993*, June 1996, NCJ 148823.

• *Law Enforcement Management and Administrative Statistics, 1993: Data for Individual State and Local Agencies with 100 or More Officers*, September 1995, NCJ 148825.

The titles for the BJS publications containing the 1997 data are the same except for the year designation.

• *Law Enforcement Management and Administrative Statistics, 1997: Data for Individual State and Local Agencies with 100 or More Officers*, April 1999, NCJ 171681.

• *Local Police Departments, 1997*, February 2000, NCJ 173429.

• *Sheriffs' Departments, 1997*, February 2000, NCJ 173428.

According to these publications, the racial make-up of the Nation's police force changed only slightly from 1993 to 1997 (1% drop in "white" and 1% rise in "other races"). In 1993, 88% of all police officers were white, 11% were black, and 1% were other races. In 1997, the comparable figures were 87% white, 11% black, and 2% other races. The percentages given in this report for the racial classification of the police force in 1998 and in the 1990's are based on the 1997 statistics. Note that officers designated "Hispanic" in the publications were classified as "white."

Police use of non-lethal force

To learn more about the use of force requires an understanding of the reasons for and the results of police-citizen encounters. During 1996 (and again in 1999*), the Bureau of Justice Statistics (BJS) carried out a special survey of 6,421 residents age 12 or older entitled the *Police-Public Contact Survey*.

The *Police-Public Contact Survey* has made possible, for the first time, estimates of the prevalence of all kinds of contacts between the police and members of the public, favorable as well as unfavorable. Results indicate that a small percentage of police-public contacts results in the use of force. In 1996, for example, about 45 million Americans age 12 or older (about 1 in 5 residents of this age) were estimated to have had at least one face-to-face contact with a police officer. Of these, about 500,000 (about 1 in 500 residents age 12 or older) were estimated to have experienced force or threat of force by police during 1996.

---
*Findings from the *1999 Police-Public Contact Survey* were published in January 2001.

There are no official national statistical data on the number of times police were justified in using lethal force (during violent and mass rioting, for example), but instead used less-than-lethal force. (For example, rather than using bullets, police can use a weapon that fires small beanbags or hard plastic rounds from a shotgun; there are also foams that can be sprayed by police that literally stop offenders in their tracks).

Additional information about the police use of force can be found in the following:

Alpert, Geoffrey. *Police Pursuit Driving and the Use of Excessive Force*. NIJ Final Report, Grant No. 95-IJ-CX-0066, 1996.

Binder, Arnold; Peter Scharf; and Raymond Galvin. *Use of Deadly Force by Police Officers*. NIJ Final Report, Grant No. 79-NI-AX-0134, 1982.

Bureau of Justice Statistics. *Police Use of Force: Collection of National Data*, NCJ 165040, November 1997.

Fridell, Lorie A. and Antony M. Pate. *Death on Patrol: Felonious Homicides of American Police Officers*. NIJ Draft Final Report, Grant No. 91-IJ-CX-K025, 1995.

Garner, Joel; John Buchanan; Tom Schade; and John Hepburn. *Understanding the Use of Force By and Against the Police*. NIJ Research in Brief, 1996.

Geller, William A. and Hans Toch, eds. *And Justice for All: A National Agenda for Understanding and Controlling Police Abuse of Force*. Washington, D.C.: Police Executive Research Forum, 1995.

Matulia, Kenneth J. *A Balance of Forces*. Gaithersburg, MD: International Association of Chiefs of Police, 1982.

Pate, Antony M. and Lorie A. Fridell. *Police Use of Force: Official Reports, Citizen Complaints, and Legal Consequences, Volumes I and II.* Washington, D.C.: The Police Foundation, 1993.

Pinizzotto, Anthony J.; Edward F. Davis; and Charles E. Miller III. *In the Line of Fire: A Study of Selected Felonious Assaults on Law Enforcement Officers.* Washington, D.C.: U.S. Department of Justice, 1997.

Scrivner, Ellen M. *The Role of Police Psychology in Controlling Excessive Force.* NIJ Research Report, NCJ-146206, 1994.

A new source of data on police officers killed and assaulted

A growing number of law enforcement agencies are adopting a new type of record keeping system — called National Incident Based Reporting System or NIBRS — for compiling crime statistics. While NIBRS data cannot distinguish nonjustifiable homicides by police from other nonjustifiable homicides, these data do provide a source of various statistics on justifiable homicides by police; for example, the number of justifiable homicides by police occurring as a result of attacking the officer, or fleeing from a crime, or resisting arrest, or committing a crime. NIBRS data also provide a source of statistics on murders of, or assaults on, law enforcement officers.

NIBRS records also have information about other offenses that were committed as part of the same incident (if any), other arrestees (if any), and additional victims (if any).

Bureau of Justice Statistics reports that use NIBRS data include:

Effects of NIBRS on Crime Statistics (BJS 7/2000, NCJ 178890)

Sexual Assault of Young Children as Reported to Law Enforcement: Victim, Incident, and Offender Characteristics (BJS 7/2000, NCJ 182990)

Office of Juvenile Justice and Delinquency Prevention reports that use NIBRS data include:

Characteristics of Crimes Against Juveniles (OJJDP 6/2000, NCJ 179034)

Kidnaping of Juveniles: Patterns From NIBRS (OJJDP 6/2000, NCJ 181161)

To obtain copies of these reports, please contact the National Criminal Justice Reference Service (NCJRS) at 1-800-732-3277 or at http://www.ncjrs.org/.

Data for figure 1. Felons killed by police in justifiable homicides, 1976-98

Year	Total number of justifiable homicides
Annual average	373
1976	415
1977	311
1978	313
1979	442
1980	457
1981	381
1982	376
1983	406
1984	332
1985	321
1986	298
1987	296
1988	339
1989	362
1990	379
1991	359
1992	414
1993	453
1994	459
1995	382
1996	355
1997	361
1998	367

Note: Data shown in table do not include justifiable homicides by police for the following years and States: 1988, Florida, Kentucky; 1989, Florida; 1990, Florida; 1991, Florida; 1993, Kansas; 1994, Kansas; 1995, Illinois, Kansas; 1996, District of Columbia; Kansas 1997, Florida, Kansas; 1998, District of Columbia, Florida, Kansas, Wisconsin.
Source: FBI database, *Supplementary Homicide Reports.*

Data for figure 2. Felons killed by police in justifiable homicides: Rate per 1 million U.S. population age 13 or older, 1976-98

Year	Total number of justifiable homicides	U.S. resident population age 13 or older on July 1	Rate of justifiable homicides (per million)
Annual average	373		1.90
1976	415	172,563,000	2.40
1977	311	175,420,000	1.77
1978	313	178,188,000	1.76
1979	442	180,793,000	2.44
1980	457	183,258,000	2.49
1981	381	185,255,000	2.06
1982	376	187,588,000	2.00
1983	406	189,782,000	2.14
1984	332	191,992,000	1.73
1985	321	194,085,000	1.65
1986	298	195,905,000	1.52
1987	296	197,545,000	1.50
1988	339	199,252,000	1.70
1989	362	200,911,000	1.80
1990	379	201,938,000	1.88
1991	359	203,849,000	1.76
1992	414	206,047,000	2.01
1993	453	208,335,000	2.17
1994	459	210,468,000	2.18
1995	382	212,588,000	1.80
1996	355	214,769,000	1.65
1997	361	217,391,000	1.66
1998	367	219,801,000	1.67

Note: Data shown in table do not include justifiable homicides by police for the following years and States: 1988, Florida, Kentucky; 1989, Florida; 1990, Florida; 1991, Florida; 1993, Kansas; 1994, Kansas; 1995, Illinois, Kansas; 1996, District of Columbia, Kansas; 1997, Florida, Kansas; 1998, District of Columbia, Florida, Kansas, Wisconsin.
Populations include States that did not report justifiable homicides.
Source: FBI database, *Supplementary Homicide Reports.*

Data for figure 3. Gender of felons killed by police in justifiable homicides: Rate per 10 million population age 13 or older, 1976-98

Year	Total number of justifiable homicides	U.S. resident population age 13 or older on July 1			Male felons			Female felons		
		Total	Male	Female	Number	Percent	Rate per 10 million	Number	Percent	Rate per 10 million
Annual average	373				364	97.7%	39	9	2.3%	1
1976	415	172,563,000	82,883,000	89,680,000	410	98.8%	49	5	1.2%	1
1977	311	175,420,000	84,234,000	91,186,000	305	98.1	36	6	1.9	1
1978	313	178,188,000	85,527,000	92,661,000	307	98.1	36	6	1.9	1
1979	442	180,793,000	86,757,000	94,036,000	430	97.3	50	12	2.7	1
1980	457	183,258,000	87,928,000	95,330,000	447	97.8%	51	10	2.2%	1
1981	381	185,255,000	88,894,000	96,361,000	378	99.2	43	3	0.8	0
1982	376	187,588,000	90,015,000	97,573,000	369	98.1	41	7	1.9	1
1983	406	189,782,000	91,105,000	98,677,000	402	99.0	44	4	1.0	0
1984	332	191,992,000	92,167,000	99,825,000	325	97.9	35	7	2.1	1
1985	321	194,085,000	93,302,000	100,783,000	314	97.8%	34	7	2.2%	1
1986	298	195,905,000	94,235,000	101,670,000	294	98.7	31	4	1.3	0
1987	296	197,545,000	95,053,000	102,492,000	290	98.0	31	6	2.0	1
1988	339	199,252,000	95,902,000	103,350,000	333	98.2	35	6	1.8	1
1989	362	200,911,000	96,730,000	104,181,000	347	95.9	36	15	4.1	1
1990	379	201,938,000	97,325,000	104,613,000	366	96.6%	38	13	3.4%	1
1991	359	203,849,000	98,222,000	105,627,000	344	95.8	35	15	4.2	1
1992	414	206,047,000	99,358,000	106,689,000	405	97.8	41	9	2.2	1
1993	453	208,335,000	100,499,000	107,836,000	439	96.9	44	14	3.1	1
1994	459	210,468,000	101,549,000	108,919,000	440	95.9	43	19	4.1	2
1995	382	212,588,000	102,630,000	109,958,000	377	98.7%	37	5	1.3%	0
1996	355	214,759,000	103,722,000	111,037,000	347	97.7	33	8	2.3	1
1997	361	217,391,000	104,995,000	112,396,000	349	96.7	33	12	3.3	1
1998	367	219,801,000	106,210,000	113,591,000	358	97.5	34	9	2.5	1

Note: "Total number" includes all instances of justifiable homicide by police whether or not the demographic characteristics are known. The felon's gender is known in 99.9% of the justifiable homicides by police between 1976 and 1998.
Populations include States that did not report justifiable homicides.
Due to rounding error, population detail may not sum to total.
Source: FBI database, *Supplementary Homicide Reports.*

Data for figure 4. Race of felons killed by police in justifiable homicides: Percent white, black, and other, 1976-98

Year	Total number of justifiable homicides	Percent of killed felons		
		White	Black	Other
Annual average	373	56%	42%	2%
1976	415	46%	52%	2%
1977	311	47	51	2
1978	313	50	49	1
1979	442	50	48	2
1980	457	51%	48%	1%
1981	381	54	45	1
1982	376	52	46	2
1983	406	54	44	2
1984	332	58	41	1
1985	321	61%	35%	4%
1986	298	58	40	2
1987	296	64	34	2
1988	339	59	39	2
1989	362	60	38	2
1990	379	62%	36%	2%
1991	359	54	43	3
1992	414	60	38	2
1993	453	55	42	3
1994	459	57	40	3
1995	382	59%	38%	3%
1996	355	61	37	2
1997	361	63	35	2
1998	367	62	35	3

Note: "Total number" includes all instances of justifiable homicide by police whether or not the demographic characteristics are known. The felon's race is known in 99.3% of the justifiable homicides by police between 1976 and 1998.
Source: FBI database, *Supplementary Homicide Reports*.

Data for figure 5. Race of felons killed by police in justifiable homicides:
Rate per 1 million population age 13 or older, 1976-98

Year	Total number of justifiable homicides	Felon's race			U.S. resident population age 13 or older on July 1				Rate of justifiable homicide (per million age 13 or older)			
		White	Black	Other	Total	White	Black	Other	Total	White	Black	Other
Annual average	373	208	155	7					1.90	1.24	7.02	1.23
1976	415	193	215	7	172,563,000	151,219,000	18,494,000	2,850,000	2.40	1.28	11.63	2.46
1977	311	148	158	5	175,420,000	153,451,000	18,937,000	3,032,000	1.77	0.96	8.34	1.65
1978	313	156	155	2	178,188,000	155,582,000	19,381,000	3,225,000	1.76	1.00	8.00	0.62
1979	442	221	213	8	180,793,000	157,553,000	19,791,000	3,449,000	2.44	1.40	10.76	2.32
1980	457	229	217	3	183,258,000	159,147,000	20,148,000	3,963,000	2.49	1.44	10.77	0.76
1981	381	205	172	3	185,255,000	160,557,000	20,498,000	4,200,000	2.06	1.28	8.39	0.71
1982	376	192	172	7	187,588,000	162,022,000	20,961,000	4,605,000	2.00	1.19	8.21	1.52
1983	406	216	177	7	189,782,000	163,610,000	21,325,000	4,847,000	2.14	1.32	8.30	1.44
1984	332	191	136	4	191,992,000	165,143,000	21,728,000	5,121,000	1.73	1.16	6.26	0.78
1985	321	195	113	12	194,085,000	166,604,000	22,056,000	5,425,000	1.65	1.17	5.12	2.21
1986	298	170	119	5	195,905,000	167,785,000	22,400,000	5,720,000	1.52	1.01	5.31	0.87
1987	296	188	100	5	197,545,000	168,824,000	22,711,000	6,010,000	1.50	1.11	4.40	0.83
1988	339	196	132	6	199,252,000	169,909,000	23,031,000	6,312,000	1.70	1.15	5.73	0.95
1989	362	217	136	6	200,911,000	170,984,000	23,326,000	6,601,000	1.80	1.27	5.83	0.91
1990	379	232	135	8	201,938,000	171,178,000	23,299,000	7,461,000	1.88	1.36	5.79	1.07
1991	359	190	154	12	203,849,000	172,450,000	23,657,000	7,742,000	1.76	1.10	6.51	1.55
1992	414	245	155	9	206,047,000	173,906,000	24,081,000	8,060,000	2.01	1.41	6.44	1.12
1993	453	246	191	13	208,335,000	175,451,000	24,506,000	8,378,000	2.17	1.40	7.79	1.55
1994	459	261	185	12	210,468,000	176,901,000	24,899,000	8,668,000	2.18	1.48	7.43	1.38
1995	382	226	143	10	212,588,000	178,363,000	25,292,000	8,933,000	1.80	1.27	5.65	1.12
1996	355	218	130	7	214,759,000	179,835,000	25,679,000	9,245,000	1.65	1.21	5.06	0.76
1997	361	226	127	6	217,391,000	181,480,000	26,159,000	9,752,000	1.66	1.25	4.85	0.62
1998	367	225	127	12	219,801,000	183,098,000	26,605,000	10,098,000	1.67	1.23	4.77	1.19

Note: "Total number" includes all instances of justifiable homicide by police whether
or not the demographic characteristics are known. The felon's race is known
in 99.3% of the justifiable homicides by police between 1976 and 1998.
Populations include States that did not report justifiable homicides.
Source: FBI database, *Supplementary Homicide Reports*.

Data for figure 6. Race of felons arrested for violent crime: Rate per 100,000 population age 13 or older, 1976-98

Year	U.S. resident population age 13 or older on July 1		Estimated number of arrests for violent crime		Rate (per 100,000) of arrest for violent crime	
	White	Black	White	Black	White	Black
Annual average			257,020	220,159	188	1,197
1976	151,219,000	18,494,000	207,648	195,636	137	1,058
1977	153,451,000	18,937,000	227,278	199,077	148	1,051
1978	155,582,000	19,381,000	300,752	276,525	193	1,427
1979	157,553,000	19,791,000	251,094	206,387	159	1,043
1980	159,147,000	20,148,000	258,574	209,707	162	1,041
1981	160,557,000	20,498,000	259,795	224,142	162	1,093
1982	162,022,000	20,961,000	273,035	245,971	169	1,173
1983	163,610,000	21,325,000	255,579	236,967	156	1,111
1984	165,143,000	21,728,000	262,591	225,171	159	1,036
1985	166,604,000	22,056,000	256,471	234,195	154	1,062
1986	167,785,000	22,400,000	289,206	257,404	172	1,149
1987	168,824,000	22,711,000	279,711	258,664	166	1,139
1988	169,909,000	23,031,000	323,684	292,691	191	1,271
1989	170,984,000	23,326,000	348,181	327,083	204	1,402
1990	171,178,000	23,299,000	284,759	274,860	166	1,180
1991	172,450,000	23,657,000	385,494	321,805	224	1,360
1992	173,906,000	24,081,000	397,809	332,674	229	1,381
1993	175,451,000	24,506,000	396,288	344,841	226	1,407
1994	176,901,000	24,899,000	415,725	348,301	235	1,399
1995	178,363,000	25,292,000	432,623	347,664	243	1,375
1996	179,835,000	25,679,000	398,612	315,070	222	1,227
1997	181,480,000	26,159,000	407,926	295,092	225	1,128
1998	183,098,000	26,605,000	390,044	271,823	213	1,022

Source: FBI, *Uniform Crime Reports.*

Data for figure 7. Age of felons killed by police in justifiable homicides: Rate per 1 million population that age, 1976-98

Year	Total number of justifiable homicides	Total rate of justifiable homicides	Rate of justifiable homicide per 1 million									
			13-19	20-24	25-29	30-34	35-39	40-44	45-49	50-54	55-59	60 or older
Annual average	373	1.90	1.58	3.96*	3.84	3.07	2.24	1.70	1.19	0.77	0.61	0.29
1976	415	2.40	2.04	5.10	5.50	3.67	2.69	1.61	1.12	0.75	0.92	0.43
1977	311	1.77	1.24	3.74	3.58	2.49	2.44	2.23	1.57	0.34	0.71	0.27
1978	313	1.76	1.53	3.76	2.91	2.40	2.60	2.21	0.79	0.85	0.53	0.32
1979	442	2.44	1.96	5.02	4.87	3.77	2.80	1.48	2.23	0.77	0.86	0.40
1980	457	2.49	1.79	5.51	5.04	4.45	3.41	1.53	1.00	0.86	0.86	0.25
1981	381	2.06	1.63	3.64	4.83	3.04	2.71	1.25	1.55	0.78	0.34	0.38
1982	376	2.00	1.33	3.80	4.70	3.36	2.25	1.51	1.18	0.52	0.43	0.40
1983	406	2.14	1.17	3.82	4.03	3.89	2.15	3.80	0.36	1.52	0.44	0.42
1984	332	1.73	1.25	3.61	3.24	2.65	1.96	1.81	1.49	0.91	0.44	0.23
1985	321	1.65	0.85	3.24	3.68	2.37	1.98	1.21	1.03	0.73	0.71	0.43
1986	298	1.52	1.10	2.45	2.86	2.84	1.60	1.05	0.75	0.92	0.44	0.27
1987	296	1.50	0.80	3.28	2.46	2.16	2.13	1.61	1.05	0.73	0.99	0.22
1988	339	1.70	1.29	2.76	3.79	2.94	1.99	1.74	1.07	0.72	0.73	0.17
1989	362	1.80	1.39	3.58	3.69	3.03	1.89	1.66	1.33	1.32	0.75	0.12
1990	379	1.88	1.35	3.66	4.05	2.97	2.25	1.80	1.59	0.79	0.19	0.24
1991	359	1.76	2.17	3.65	3.71	2.93	1.61	1.55	0.78	0.52	0.48	0.17
1992	414	2.01	2.12	4.83	4.26	2.92	2.09	1.70	1.30	0.50	0.29	0.21
1993	453	2.17	2.53	4.95	3.92	3.28	2.23	2.08	1.07	0.94	0.75	0.42
1994	459	2.18	2.19	5.23	4.06	3.43	2.69	1.78	1.50	0.68	0.91	0.35
1995	382	1.80	1.87	4.59	2.95	3.38	2.02	1.43	1.03	0.59	0.45	0.21
1996	355	1.65	1.75	3.80	3.21	3.04	1.73	1.35	1.14	0.43	0.62	0.27
1997	361	1.66	1.42	3.37	3.40	2.85	2.39	1.22	1.19	0.79	0.85	0.25
1998	367	1.67	1.58	3.62	3.50	2.82	1.86	1.51	1.22	0.83	0.24	0.29

Note: "Total number" includes all instances of justifiable homicide by police whether or not the demographic characteristics are known. The felon's age is known in 98.7% of the justifiable homicides by police between 1976 and 1998. The 13-19 age category includes one 11-year-old in 1981 and one 12-year-old in 1992.
Populations include States that did not report justifiable homicides.
*Population denominators for rates are available in Appendix table 1.
Source: FBI database, *Supplementary Homicide Reports*.

Data for figure 8. Felons killed by police in justifiable homicide: Percent under and over age 25, by race and gender, 1976-98

Year	Total number of justifiable homicides	Percent of killed felons under age 25*						Percent of killed felons age 25 or older					
		Male			Female			Male			Female		
		White	Black	Other race	White	Black	Other race	White	Black	Other race	White	Black	Other race
Annual average	373	16%	16%	1%	0%	0%	0%	39%	25%	1%	1%	1%	0%
1976	415	19%	20%	0%	0%	0%	0%	27%	32%	1%	1%	0%	0%
1977	311	16	19	0	0	1	0	32	30	1	0	1	0
1978	313	19	20	0	0	0	0	30	29	0	1	1	0
1979	442	18	18	1	0	0	0	32	28	1	1	1	0
1980	457	20%	17%	0%	0%	0%	0%	31%	30%	0%	1%	1%	0%
1981	381	16	17	0	0	0	0	38	27	1	0	1	0
1982	376	17	14	1	0	0	0	33	32	1	1	1	0
1983	406	12	15	1	0	0	0	41	29	1	0	1	0
1984	332	19	14	0	0	0	0	38	27	1	1	0	0
1985	321	15%	13%	1%	0%	0%	0%	45%	22%	1%	2%	1%	0%
1986	298	17	13	1	0	0	0	40	27	1	1	0	0
1987	296	17	11	0	0	0	0	47	22	1	1	1	0
1988	339	11	12	1	1	0	0	46	27	1	1	0	0
1989	362	15	12	1	1	0	0	43	23	1	2	2	0
1990	379	14%	13%	1%	0%	0%	0%	47%	21%	1%	1%	2%	0%
1991	359	16	15	2	0	1	0	35	26	1	2	1	1
1992	414	17	17	1	1	0	0	41	21	1	1	0	0
1993	453	13	20	1	0	0	0	42	21	1	1	1	0
1994	459	16	15	1	1	0	0	38	24	2	2	1	0
1995	382	17%	17%	1%	0%	0%	0%	42%	20%	2%	1%	0%	0%
1996	355	15	16	1	0	0	0	46	20	1	1	0	0
1997	361	12	14	1	0	0	0	49	20	1	2	1	0
1998	367	15	14	1	0	0	0	45	21	2	1	1	0

Note: "Total number" includes all instances of justifiable homicide by police whether or not the demographic characteristics are known. The felon's age, gender, and race are all known in 98.1% of the justifiable homicides by police between 1976 and 1998.
*Felons under age 25 refers only to persons ages 13-24.
Source: FBI database, *Supplementary Homicide Reports*.

Data for figure 9. Race, gender, and age of felons killed by police in justifiable homicides: Rate per 1 million U.S. population under age 25 and 25 or older, 1980-98

Year	Total rate	Rate of killed felons under age 25* Male White	Black	Other race	Female White	Black	Other race	Rate of killed felons age 25 or older Male White	Black	Other race	Female White	Black	Other race
Annual average	1.86	2.93	16.50	3.01	0.06	0.11	0.11	2.36	12.29	1.96	0.06	0.33	0.03
1980	2.49	4.10	22.84	1.66	0.10	0.00	0.00	2.45	22.09	1.50	0.06	0.54	0.00
1981	2.06	2.78	18.49	0.00	0.00	0.00	0.00	2.56	16.85	2.21	0.00	0.40	0.00
1982	2.00	2.91	15.60	4.27	0.00	0.00	0.00	2.15	18.63	2.71	0.06	0.39	0.00
1983	2.14	2.27	18.02	4.05	0.00	0.00	0.00	2.80	17.67	2.51	0.02	0.38	0.00
1984	1.73	2.97	13.58	1.28	0.05	0.00	0.00	2.11	13.26	1.76	0.06	0.12	0.00
1985	1.65	2.28	12.44	2.42	0.00	0.00	0.00	2.32	10.10	5.47	0.07	0.24	0.00
1986	1.52	2.43	11.04	2.29	0.05	0.00	0.00	1.89	11.44	1.54	0.03	0.12	0.00
1987	1.50	2.54	9.97	1.10	0.05	0.30	0.00	2.13	8.90	1.92	0.03	0.23	0.00
1988	1.70	1.96	12.21	2.11	0.17	0.00	0.00	2.42	12.28	1.35	0.03	0.11	0.00
1989	1.80	2.86	13.58	2.02	0.11	0.00	0.00	2.42	11.34	1.70	0.08	0.77	0.00
1990	1.88	2.88	15.39	1.97	0.00	0.00	1.05	2.67	10.11	1.92	0.07	0.75	0.00
1991	1.76	3.19	16.98	5.78	0.06	0.63	0.00	1.87	11.95	1.47	0.10	0.32	0.66
1992	2.01	3.76	21.16	4.69	0.18	0.00	0.00	2.53	10.56	1.40	0.07	0.10	0.00
1993	2.17	3.19	26.72	5.48	0.06	0.31	0.95	2.71	11.46	2.01	0.08	0.51	0.00
1994	2.18	4.03	21.26	4.47	0.18	0.30	0.00	2.56	13.31	2.26	0.15	0.40	0.00
1995	1.80	3.35	19.54	2.63	0.06	0.00	0.00	2.27	9.02	2.18	0.04	0.10	0.00
1996	1.65	2.79	16.42	4.32	0.06	0.30	0.00	2.30	8.26	0.60	0.07	0.10	0.00
1997	1.66	2.49	14.20	3.39	0.00	0.00	0.00	2.45	8.21	0.58	0.09	0.38	0.00
1998	1.67	2.89	14.00	3.32	0.00	0.29	0.00	2.25	8.05	2.22	0.07	0.28	0.00

Note: "Total rate" column includes all instances of justifiable homicide by police whether or not the demographic characteristics are known. The felon's race, gender, and age are all known in 98.1% of the justifiable homicides by police between 1980 and 1998.
Populations include States that did not report justifiable homicides.
*Felons under age 25 refers only to persons ages 13-24.
Population denominators are available in Appendix table 2.
Source: FBI database, *Supplementary Homicide Reports*.

Data for figure 10. Race of police officers who killed felons in justifiable homicides: Percent white, black, and other, 1976-98

Year	Total number of justifiable homicides by police	Percent of officers		
		White	Black	Other
Annual average	373	84%	15%	1%
1976	415	82%	16%	2%
1977	311	83	17	0
1978	313	85	15	0
1979	442	83	16	1
1980	457	86%	14%	0%
1981	381	87	13	0
1982	376	86	14	0
1983	406	90	9	1
1984	332	86	12	2
1985	321	85%	13%	2%
1986	298	90	10	0
1987	296	86	12	2
1988	339	86	13	1
1989	362	87	13	0
1990	379	83%	16%	1%
1991	359	81	18	1
1992	414	82	16	2
1993	453	82	17	1
1994	459	77	22	1
1995	382	84%	15%	1%
1996	355	87	12	1
1997	361	81	17	2
1998	367	82	17	1

Note: "Total number" includes all instances of justifiable homicide by police whether or not the demographic characteristics are known. The officer's race is known in 77.2% of the justifiable homicides by police between 1976 and 1998.
Source: FBI database, *Supplementary Homicide Reports*.

Data for figure 11. Race of felons and police officers in justifiable homicides: Number and percent interracial and intraracial, 1976-98

Year	Total number of justifiable homicides by police	Officer is white, felon is —		Officer is black, felon is —	
		White	Black	White	Black
Annual average	373	53%	30%	3%	12%
1976	415	41%	41%	2%	14%
1977	311	43	38	3	15
1978	313	46	38	2	14
1979	442	46	35	3	13
1980	457	50%	35%	1%	13%
1981	381	51	34	2	12
1982	376	46	39	1	13
1983	406	52	36	1	8
1984	332	53	32	3	9
1985	321	58%	25%	5%	8%
1986	298	56	31	2	8
1987	296	60	25	5	7
1988	339	57	27	3	10
1989	362	60	25	2	11
1990	379	56%	24%	5%	12%
1991	359	55	23	2	16
1992	414	56	24	4	12
1993	453	53	26	3	14
1994	459	54	22	2	20
1995	382	57%	26%	2%	12%
1996	355	57	28	3	8
1997	361	58	22	4	13
1998	367	56	24	5	12

Note: "Total number" includes all instances of justifiable homicide by police whether or not the demographic characteristics are known. The officer's race is known in 76.9% of the justifiable homicides by police between 1976 and 1998. The felon's race is known in 99.3% of the justifiable homicides by police between 1976 and 1998.
Detail does not sum to 100% because table does not show all racial combinations.
Source: FBI database, *Supplementary Homicide Reports*.

Data for figure 12. Number of police officers murdered by felons, 1976-98	
Year	Total number of officers murdered
Annual average	79
1976	111
1977	93
1978	93
1979	106
1980	104
1981	91
1982	92
1983	80
1984	72
1985	78
1986	66
1987	74
1988	78
1989	66
1990	66
1991	71
1992	64
1993	70
1994	79
1995	74
1996	61
1997	70
1998	61

Source: FBI, *Law Enforcement Officers Killed and Assaulted.*

Data for figure 13. Number of police officers murdered by felons compared to felons killed by police in justifiable homicides, 1976-98		
Year	Officers murdered	Felons killed
Annual average	79	373
1976	111	415
1977	93	311
1978	93	313
1979	106	442
1980	104	457
1981	91	381
1982	92	376
1983	80	406
1984	72	332
1985	78	321
1986	66	298
1987	74	296
1988	78	339
1989	66	362
1990	66	379
1991	71	359
1992	64	414
1993	70	453
1994	79	459
1995	74	382
1996	61	355
1997	70	361
1998	61	367

Source: FBI, *Law Enforcement Officers Killed and Assaulted*, and FBI database, *Supplementary Homicide Reports.*

Data for figure 14. Police officers murdered by felons: Rate per 100,000 officers, 1976-98

Year	Total number of officers murdered	Total number of sworn police	Rate per 100,000	Approximately 1 of every —
Annual average	79		17.1	6,503
1976	111	391,895	28.3	3,531
1977	93	384,816	24.2	4,138
1978	93	391,751	23.7	4,212
1979	106	373,605	28.4	3,525
1980	104	393,363	26.4	3,782
1981	91	398,064	22.9	4,374
1982	92	403,407	22.8	4,385
1983	80	449,370	17.8	5,617
1984	72	467,117	15.4	6,488
1985	78	470,678	16.6	6,034
1986	66	475,853	13.9	7,210
1987	74	480,383	15.2	6,492
1988	78	485,566	16.1	6,225
1989	66	496,353	13.3	7,521
1990	66	523,262	12.6	7,928
1991	71	535,629	13.3	7,544
1992	64	544,309	11.4	8,505
1993	70	553,773	12.6	7,911
1994	79	561,543	13.5	7,108
1995	74	586,756	12.6	7,929
1996	61	595,170	10.2	9,757
1997	70	618,127	11.3	8,830
1998	61	641,208	9.5	10,512

Source: FBI, *Law Enforcement Officers Killed and Assaulted.*

Data for figure 15. Race of police officers murdered by felons: Percent white, black, and other, 1976-98

Year	Percent of murdered officers		
	White	Black	Other
Annual average	86%	13%	1%
1976	90%	8%	2%
1977	90	10	0
1978	91	9	0
1979	88	9	3
1980	87%	13%	0%
1981	85	14	1
1982	84	15	1
1983	83	13	4
1984	85	14	1
1985	89%	10%	1%
1986	89	11	0
1987	90	10	0
1988	91	9	0
1989	89	11	0
1990	80%	18%	2%
1991	87	13	0
1992	82	16	2
1993	86	14	0
1994	84	15	1
1995	84%	12%	4%
1996	80	15	5
1997	80	17	3
1998	87	11	2

Source: FBI, *Law Enforcement Officers Killed and Assaulted.*

Data for figure 16. Felons who murdered police officers:
Percent with criminal history, 1976-98

Year	Any criminal act	Any narcotic drug law violation	Prior arrest for — Any violent crime	Murder charge	Weapons violation	Assaulting police or resisting arrest	Prior conviction	On parole or probation at time of killing
Annual average	67%	24%	32%	4%	28%	11%	48%	21%
1976	60%	18%	25%	5%	16%	4%	44%	23%
1977	61	15	31	3	16	3	46	4
1978	62	9	24	5	21	9	50	23
1979	63	13	43	8	30	6	49	16
1980	73%	26%	48%	6%	36%	9%	49%	25%
1981	73	26	47	7	46	14	54	26
1982	73	22	29	6	36	11	50	25
1983	72	14	11	3	22	9	40	24
1984	83	20	24	6	24	8	70	25
1985	75%	22%	19%	2%	22%	9%	51%	23%
1986	69	27	23	5	20	5	30	22
1987	54	24	26	1	20	5	49	22
1988	67	20	29	4	15	5	36	24
1989	67	17	35	7	30	14	49	12
1990	78%	33%	46%	6%	49%	14%	68%	31%
1991	60	30	28	1	18	8	46	23
1992	59	20	38	4	32	8	46	15
1993	66	31	24	4	33	18	37	14
1994	58	25	43	4	39	24	39	17
1995	69%	38%	48%	1%	31%	22%	42%	18%
1996	58	24	38	1	34	15	51	24
1997	76	44	32	1	37	18	72	24
1998	71	33	24	7	21	9	44	12

Source: FBI, *Law Enforcement Officers Killed and Assaulted.*

Data for figure 17. Felons who murdered police officers:
Percent under and over age 25, by race and gender, 1980-98

Year	Percent under age 25*						Percent age 25 or older					
	Male			Female			Male			Female		
	White	Black	Other race	White	Black	Other race	White	Black	Other race	White	Black	Other race
Annual average	20%	21%	1%	1%	1%	0%	31%	19%	2%	1%	1%	0%
1980	26%	19%	0%	3%	2%	0%	26%	22%	0%	1%	1%	0%
1981	12	20	1	0	1	0	25	38	1	2	0	0
1982	21	25	0	0	1	0	35	14	1	3	0	0
1983	22	13	1	0	0	0	42	17	4	0	1	0
1984	20	19	3	2	0	0	29	22	3	1	0	0
1985	18%	22%	3%	1%	1%	0%	25%	29%	0%	1%	0%	0%
1986	26	10	0	0	1	0	35	24	2	1	1	0
1987	20	13	4	4	0	0	37	17	1	2	1	0
1988	29	19	2	0	1	0	25	21	1	1	1	0
1989	7	21	0	1	1	0	46	21	1	0	0	1
1990	18%	18%	0%	1%	1%	0%	35%	24%	1%	0%	2%	0%
1991	21	37	0	0	0	0	35	6	1	0	0	0
1992	25	23	1	0	0	0	27	23	0	0	1	0
1993	21	39	0	0	0	0	20	19	0	1	0	0
1994	25	23	0	2	1	0	26	18	3	1	1	0
1995	20%	27%	1%	3%	1%	0%	28%	11%	3%	3%	0%	0%
1996	14	30	5	0	0	0	28	20	1	1	0	0
1997	10	15	7	0	0	0	42	15	7	0	0	0
1998	26	17	3	1	0	0	33	16	3	1	0	0

Note: Data on the race, gender, and age of felons who murder police officers are not available prior to 1980.
The felon's race, gender, and age are all known for 94.4% of felons who murdered police between 1980 and 1998.
*Felons under age 25 refers only to persons ages 13-24.
Source: FBI, *Law Enforcement Officers Killed and Assaulted.*

**Data for figure 18. Race and gender of felons who murdered police officers:
Rate per 1 million U.S. population, 1980-98**

| Year | Rate per 1 million under age 25* | | | | | | Rate per 1 million age 25 or older | | | | | |
| | Male | | | Female | | | Male | | | Female | | |
	White	Black	Other race	White	Black	Other race	White	Black	Other race	White	Black	Other race
Annual average	1.12	6.30	1.53	0.06	0.19	0.00	0.48	2.84	0.68	0.02	0.06	0.02
1980	2.03	9.19	0.00	0.24	0.86	0.00	0.78	6.19	0.00	0.02	0.27	0.00
1981	0.75	7.63	1.52	0.00	0.28	0.00	0.57	8.09	0.74	0.05	0.00	0.00
1982	1.19	8.83	0.00	0.00	0.29	0.00	0.72	2.57	0.68	0.06	0.00	0.00
1983	1.11	4.14	1.35	0.00	0.00	0.00	0.76	2.81	2.51	0.00	0.13	0.00
1984	0.93	5.31	3.83	0.10	0.00	0.00	0.46	3.05	1.76	0.02	0.00	0.00
1985	0.99	7.11	3.62	0.05	0.29	0.00	0.45	4.75	0.00	0.01	0.00	0.00
1986	1.17	2.69	0.00	0.00	0.29	0.00	0.51	3.04	1.02	0.01	0.12	0.00
1987	0.93	3.63	4.40	0.22	0.00	0.00	0.55	2.26	0.48	0.03	0.12	0.00
1988	1.91	7.33	3.16	0.00	0.30	0.00	0.49	3.59	0.45	0.01	0.11	0.00
1989	0.32	5.25	0.00	0.06	0.31	0.00	0.59	2.29	0.42	0.00	0.00	0.38
1990	0.83	4.71	0.00	0.06	0.31	0.00	0.45	2.63	0.38	0.00	0.21	0.00
1991	1.12	11.01	0.00	0.00	0.00	0.00	0.50	0.77	0.37	0.00	0.00	0.00
1992	1.18	5.91	0.94	0.00	0.00	0.00	0.35	2.39	0.00	0.00	0.10	0.00
1993	0.95	9.52	0.00	0.00	0.00	0.00	0.24	1.85	0.00	0.01	0.00	0.00
1994	1.51	7.29	0.00	0.12	0.30	0.00	0.41	2.30	0.97	0.01	0.10	0.00
1995	1.01	7.21	0.88	0.18	0.30	0.00	0.36	1.19	0.93	0.04	0.00	0.00
1996	0.56	6.57	3.45	0.00	0.00	0.00	0.30	1.74	0.30	0.01	0.00	0.00
1997	1.66	3.25	4.24	0.00	0.00	0.00	0.43	1.25	1.44	0.00	0.00	0.00
1998	1.20	3.21	1.66	0.06	0.00	0.00	0.31	1.23	0.56	0.01	0.00	0.00

Note: Data on the race, gender, and age of felons who murder police officers are not available prior to 1980.
The felon's race, gender, and age are all known for 94.4% of felons who murdered police between 1980 and 1998.
*Felons under age 25 refers only to persons ages 13-24.
Population denominators are available in Appendix table 2.
Source: FBI, *Law Enforcement Officers Killed and Assaulted*.

Data for table 3. Age of felons killed by police in justifiable homicides, 1976-98

Year	Total number of justifiable homicides	Percent of killed felons who were ages —									
		13-19	20-24	25-29	30-34	35-39	40-44	45-49	50-54	55-59	60 or older
Annual average	373	11%	21%	21%	17%	11%	7%	4%	3%	2%	3%
1976	415	15%	25%	25%	13%	8%	4%	3%	2%	2%	3%
1977	311	12	23	21	13	10	8	6	1	3	3
1978	313	14	25	17	13	11	8	3	3	2	4
1979	442	13	25	21	15	9	4	6	2	2	3
1980	457	11%	27%	22%	17%	11%	4%	2%	2%	2%	2%
1981	381	12	21	26	15	10	4	5	2	1	4
1982	376	10	22	26	17	9	5	4	2	1	4
1983	406	8	20	21	19	9	13	1	4	1	4
1984	332	10	22	21	16	10	8	5	3	2	3
1985	321	7%	22%	25%	15%	11%	5%	4%	3%	3%	5%
1986	298	10	18	22	21	11	5	3	4	2	4
1987	296	7	21	19	16	14	9	4	3	4	3
1988	339	10	16	26	19	11	8	4	2	2	2
1989	362	9	19	23	19	10	8	5	4	2	1
1990	379	9%	19%	22%	17%	12%	9%	6%	2%	1%	3%
1991	359	15	20	22	18	9	8	3	2	1	2
1992	414	13	22	21	16	11	8	5	1	1	2
1993	453	14	20	17	16	11	9	4	3	2	4
1994	459	12	21	17	17	13	8	5	2	2	3
1995	382	13%	22%	15%	20%	12%	8%	5%	2%	1%	2%
1996	355	13	19	17	19	11	8	6	2	2	3
1997	361	11	17	18	17	15	7	6	3	3	3
1998	367	12	18	18	16	12	9	6	4	1	4

Note: "Total number" includes all instances of justifiable homicide by police whether or not the demographic characteristics are known. The felon's age is known in 98.7% of the justifiable homicides by police between 1976 and 1998.
The 13-19 age category includes one 11-year-old in 1981 and one 12-year-old in 1992.
Source: FBI database, *Supplementary Homicide Reports*.

Data for table 6. Age of police officers who killed felons in justifiable homicides, 1976-98

Year	Total number of justifiable homicides by police	Percent of officers who were ages —											
		Under 20	20-24	25-29	30-34	35-39	40-44	45-49	50-54	55-59	60-64	65-69	70 or older
Annual average	373	1%	9%	28%	28%	17%	10%	4%	2%	0%	0%	0%	0%
1976	415	0%	10%	37%	30%	10%	5%	4%	2%	0%	1%	1%	0%
1977	311	0	11	39	28	10	4	3	3	1	1	0	0
1978	313	1	13	35	32	12	5	1	1	0	0	0	0
1979	442	0	9	30	29	16	9	4	2	0	1	0	0
1980	457	0%	9%	31%	34%	17%	5%	2%	1%	1%	0%	0%	0%
1981	381	0	13	26	31	18	8	2	1	1	0	0	0
1982	376	0	7	30	32	19	6	4	1	1	0	0	0
1983	406	0	11	24	28	19	12	3	2	1	0	0	0
1984	332	0	10	22	31	23	10	3	1	0	0	0	0
1985	321	0%	7%	24%	31%	24%	8%	5%	1%	0%	0%	0%	0%
1986	298	0	7	28	28	21	13	2	1	0	0	0	0
1987	296	1	8	29	23	22	13	4	0	0	0	0	0
1988	339	0	4	25	35	18	13	3	2	0	0	0	0
1989	362	0	10	27	24	22	9	6	1	1	0	0	0
1990	379	1%	7%	26%	23%	21%	15%	5%	2%	0%	0%	0%	0%
1991	359	0	12	29	25	17	11	4	1	1	0	0	0
1992	414	0	12	25	25	16	11	8	2	1	0	0	0
1993	453	1	8	33	24	12	12	4	4	0	1	1	0
1994	459	2	8	25	28	18	12	5	2	0	0	0	0
1995	382	4%	8%	28%	26%	14%	12%	5%	2%	0%	1%	0%	0%
1996	355	0	5	31	23	15	14	9	2	1	0	0	0
1997	361	2	6	28	27	20	10	4	3	1	0	0	0
1998	367	2	7	27	27	22	8	4	2	1	0	0	0

Note: "Total number" includes all instances of justifiable homicide by police whether
or not the demographic characteristics are known. The officer's age is known in 70.1%
of the justifiable homicides by police between 1976 and 1998.
Due to rounding error, detail may not sum to 100%.
Source: FBI database, *Supplementary Homicide Reports*.

Appendix table 1. Population denominators for rates in figure 7.

Year	U.S. resident population on July 1 (in thousands)									
	13-19	20-24	25-29	30-34	35-39	40-44	45-49	50-54	55-59	60 or older
1976	29,853	19,794	18,177	14,428	11,884	11,147	11,646	11,969	10,884	32,781
1977	29,735	20,312	18,180	15,661	12,309	11,190	11,495	11,868	11,192	33,478
1978	29,483	20,748	18,586	16,218	13,052	11,321	11,352	11,814	11,425	34,189
1979	29,024	21,097	19,077	16,961	13,592	11,523	11,212	11,724	11,582	35,001
1980	28,438	21,402	19,657	17,756	14,082	11,734	11,042	11,686	11,619	35,842
1981	27,550	21,733	20,067	18,737	14,406	12,043	10,985	11,546	11,600	36,588
1982	27,085	21,560	20,649	18,754	15,567	12,558	10,992	11,447	11,519	37,457
1983	26,562	21,713	21,100	19,045	16,255	13,168	11,184	11,152	11,474	38,129
1984	26,336	21,310	21,309	19,602	16,813	13,837	11,417	11,013	11,448	38,907
1985	25,851	20,996	21,754	20,267	17,708	14,055	11,648	10,942	11,337	39,527
1986	25,422	20,415	22,010	20,774	18,723	14,345	11,927	10,887	11,268	40,134
1987	25,006	19,790	21,979	21,334	18,737	15,569	12,351	10,927	11,125	40,727
1988	24,769	19,186	21,876	21,798	19,141	16,124	13,026	11,136	10,897	41,299
1989	24,399	18,702	21,699	22,135	19,621	16,881	13,521	11,375	10,726	41,852
1990	24,385	19,136	21,234	21,906	19,975	17,789	13,819	11,368	10,474	41,852
1991	24,003	19,175	20,737	22,152	20,514	18,756	14,095	11,648	10,422	42,347
1992	24,071	19,067	20,191	22,242	21,073	18,796	15,355	12,054	10,485	42,713
1993	24,547	18,785	19,646	22,240	21,571	19,190	15,927	12,727	10,680	43,022
1994	25,088	18,351	19,206	22,164	21,938	19,687	16,674	13,191	10,933	43,236
1995	25,626	17,882	19,005	21,867	22,248	20,219	17,449	13,629	11,085	43,578
1996	26,231	17,369	19,030	21,363	22,501	20,756	18,416	13,909	11,352	43,832
1997	26,723	17,483	18,812	20,732	22,629	21,376	18,465	15,157	11,755	44,259
1998	27,172	17,674	18,588	20,186	22,626	21,894	18,859	15,725	12,407	44,670

Note: Populations include States that did not report justifiable homicides.
Population estimates are rounded and are from the U.S. Census Bureau.

Appendix table 2. Population denominators for rates in figures 9 and 18.

| Year | U.S. resident population under age 25 on July 1 (in thousands)* | | | | | | U.S. resident population age 25 or older on July 1 (in thousands) | | | | | |
| | Male | | | Female | | | Male | | | Female | | |
	White	Black	Other race	White	Black	Other race	White	Black	Other race	White	Black	Other race
1980	21,214	3,372	602	20,594	3,494	582	55,418	5,975	1,337	61,810	7,367	1,493
1981	21,243	3,408	657	20,598	3,523	629	56,164	6,055	1,355	62,642	7,467	1,513
1982	20,972	3,397	703	20,320	3,505	668	57,240	6,227	1,474	63,758	7,675	1,648
1983	20,729	3,385	741	20,038	3,481	700	58,257	6,395	1,593	64,801	7,880	1,782
1984	20,506	3,387	784	19,776	3,467	736	59,266	6,560	1,706	65,820	8,077	1,908
1985	20,163	3,375	828	19,407	3,443	775	60,320	6,735	1,828	66,882	8,287	2,041
1986	19,724	3,351	872	18,933	3,404	815	61,355	6,907	1,954	67,916	8,494	2,181
1987	19,260	3,310	910	18,440	3,354	851	62,357	7,079	2,085	68,882	8,693	2,324
1988	18,897	3,275	948	18,036	3,312	886	63,288	7,245	2,218	69,792	8,889	2,466
1989	18,543	3,239	991	17,641	3,268	927	64,175	7,408	2,358	70,663	9,084	2,616
1990	18,052	3,184	1,017	17,120	3,200	953	64,824	7,612	2,610	71,163	9,317	2,886
1991	17,862	3,179	1,037	16,954	3,194	981	65,642	7,783	2,727	71,946	9,518	3,026
1992	17,809	3,213	1,065	16,874	3,212	1,016	66,457	7,954	2,853	72,705	9,709	3,178
1993	17,853	3,254	1,094	16,921	3,247	1,054	67,188	8,112	2,977	73,410	9,895	3,330
1994	17,867	3,290	1,118	16,935	3,279	1,084	67,905	8,261	3,091	74,095	10,071	3,473
1995	17,881	3,322	1,137	16,929	3,304	1,110	68,630	8,417	3,210	74,774	10,252	3,621
1996	17,900	3,344	1,156	16,931	3,318	1,135	69,361	8,586	3,336	75,470	10,447	3,774
1997	18,061	3,380	1,180	17,072	3,349	1,165	70,135	8,772	3,467	76,213	10,658	3,940
1998	18,317	3,430	1,205	17,309	3,393	1,193	70,723	8,939	3,596	76,750	10,843	4,104

Note: Populations include States that did not report justifiable homicides.
Population estimates are rounded and are from the U.S. Census Bureau.
*Felons under age 25 refers only to persons ages 13-24.

www.ingramcontent.com/pod-product-compliance
Lightning Source LLC
Chambersburg PA
CBHW081750280526
45789CB00008B/2798